CHRONICLES OF CRIME

BOLTON

The crowd expectantly await the execution...

CHRONICLES OF CRIME

BOLTON

SARA VERNON

First published 2010

The History Press
The Mill, Brimscombe Port
Stroud, Gloucestershire, GL5 2QG
www.thehistorypress.co.uk

British Library Cataloguing in Publication Data.
A catalogue record for this book is available from the British Library.

ISBN 978 0 7524 5455 9

Typesetting and origination by The History Press
Printed in Great Britain
Manufacturing managed by Jellyfish Print Solutions Ltd

CONTENTS

RETURN of all Persons Committed, or Bailed to appear for Trial, or Indicted at the *General Quarter Session* of the peace held at *Lancaster* and by adjournment at *Preston Manchester and Rochdale* on the 30th day of *June* 1879, shewing the nature of their Offences, and the result of the Proceedings.

No.	NAMES	Offence of which those tried were Convicted or Acquitted, and of which those discharged without Trial were charged on Indictment or Commitment	Convicted and Sentenced				Acquitted and Discharged
			Death	Penal Servitude	Imprisonment; (state if also Whipped or Fined)	Term of Police Supervision	
121	Elizabeth Carr	Larceny in dwellinghouse to upwards of £in value before convicted of felony			9 Months	5 Years	
122	William Johnson	Larceny in dwellinghouse to upwards of £ in value					Acquitted
123	Peter Warren	Feloniously receiving stolen property knowing &			6 Months		
124	George Webster	Larceny			6 Months		
125	Daniel Warren	Larceny			6 Months		
126	Mary Mecham	Larceny					Acquitted
127	William Stansfield	Embezzlement as servant			9 Months		
128	John McGuire	Larceny before convicted of felony			9 Months	5 Years	
129	William Hamly	Larceny before convicted of felony			1 Year	2 Years	
130	Mary Ann Kay	Larceny			2 Months		
131	James Nuttall	Larceny					Acquitted
132	Edward Hughes	Larceny			3 Months		
133	William Foster	Embezzlement as servant & unlawfully falsifying his Accounts			18 months 1 month concurrent		
134	Ann Holden	Adjudged an incorrigible rogue			1 Year		
135	Matthew Sutcliffe	Adjudged an incorrigible rogue			1 Year		
136	Richard Leach	Indecent Assault					To give Recognizances for his good behaviour and live on terms and until she and in default to be imprisoned 3 months
137	Mary Casey	Assault			1 Month		
138	James Cummins	Assault			1 Month		
139	Michael Walsh	Unlawfully wounding			14 days		
140	Herbert Cawthorne	Unlawfully wounding			6 Months		
141	Solomon Zaporski	Assault					Recognizances in £50 to appear and receive judgment when called upon
142	Richard Pattinson	Attempting suicide					Acquitted
143	Thomas Fester	Obtaining money by false pretences Kirkdale Session 15 July 1879					Bill found - Trial postponed to next Session - bailed
144	William Wall	Embezzlement as servant			1 Year		
145	Samuel Green	Larceny					Acquitted
146	Hugh Williams	Larceny			6 Months		
147	Arthur Bolton	Shopbreaking and Larceny			3 weeks and once whipped with 12 strokes of a birch rod and on its expiration to be sent to Reformatory School for 5 years		
148	Charles Ewing	Shopbreaking and Larceny			3 weeks and once whipped with 12 strokes of a birch rod and on its expiration to be sent to Reformatory School for 5 years		
149	Thomas Leatherbarrow	Larceny before convicted of felony			6 Months	2 Years	
150	Benjamin Young	Larceny			1 Year		

Home Office Return.

It is requested that where more than one Sheet is used, each may bear a separate Heading, as the Returns are bound up as Records.

25—4

Introduction

BOLTON

The ancient parish of Bolton has an area of 33,406 acres. A very large portion of it was formerly moorland, and much still remains in this condition in the high lands in the northern half of the district. Of the formation of the parish nothing is known.

With the exception of the Pilkingtons of Rivington, the Bradshaws of Bradshaw, and the Orrells of Turton, the local landowners of the medieval period were either non-resident or obscure. 'Lusty lads, liver and light,' from Bolton-le-Moors are, in an old ballad, said to have fought at Flodden under Sir Edward Stanley. After the Reformation the district became strongly Puritan, there being very few openly avowed recusants, and it sided with the Parliament in the Civil War.

There was a dreadful visitation of the plague in 1623. Defoe, who visited the district early in the eighteenth century, 'saw nothing remarkable' in the town of Bolton, but noticed that the cotton manufacture had reached it; the place did not seem so 'nourishing' and increasing as Manchester. The later history of the parish has been that of the growth of its trade and the inventions – particularly the famous 'Crompton's mule' – by which its manufactures were able to develop to their present magnitude. The townships have (between 1894 and 1898) been greatly altered by consolidations, and the old parish now includes the following: Bolton, Little Lever, Belmont, Turton, Edgeworth, Rivington, Anglezarke, and Blackrod. The new township or civil parish of Bolton includes not only the old Great and Little Bolton, Tonge-with-Haulgh, Darcy Lever, Lostock, and the southern end of Sharpies (Sharples), but also a considerable part of the adjacent parish of Deane.

THE CHIEF CONSTABLE'S ANNUAL REPORT, 1876
(FROM THE *BOLTON JOURNAL*, 4 NOVEMBER 1876)

The annual report of Mr T. Beech (chief constable) was presented to the Watch Committee at the Borough Police Offices, Town Hall, Bolton, 25 October 1876. It revealed that, in that year:

● There were 4,258 persons proceeded against for all offences, and 208 indictable offences reported to the police (of which 160 persons were proceeded against for indictable offences, 107 were committed for trial, ten bailed for ditto, thirty-eight discharged for insufficient evidence, and five for want of prosecution).

This included:

● 170 cases of felony, including 94 cases committed for trial or summarily convicted.

● 1007 cases of drunkenness, 'in which 926 persons were concerned, fifty-two having been convicted twice during the year, eight thrice, and five four times. Thirty-four persons were discharged, nine imprisoned one month, and 392

'Types of male criminals.' Certain facial features were once considered a trait of the 'criminal types'.

imprisoned for 14 days and under, and 574 paid the fine inflicted upon them.' The estimated population was 94,500 – which gives one case of drunkenness to every ninety-four of the inhabitants. As the report puts it: 'the number of drunkards arrested on each day of the week, reckoning from 12 to 12 o'clock midnight. Sunday includes a number of drunkards, who, having become intoxicated on Saturday night on their way home, are found by the police soon after midnight, and hence they are counted in the Sunday drunkards, though really they belong to the number found drunk on the Saturday:- Sunday, 131; Monday, 139; Tuesday, 125; Wednesday, 106; Thursday, 85, Friday; 85, Saturday, 308; summoned, 30; total, 1009.'

- 80 prosecutions for assaults on the police, and 352 common assaults – including 8 cases of causing bodily harm, 7 aggravated assaults on women and children.

- 104 prosecutions against 'immoral women'.

- 1,004 people charged with breaches of the peace.

- 345 cases of parents neglecting to send their children to school.

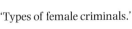
'Types of female criminals.'

- 451 people charged with offences against the local acts and borough bye-laws. 'Amongst these offenders last year there were four boys prosecuted for throwing stones to the danger, &c., of the inhabitants; this year the number has risen to 26, it having been found necessary to employ special means to detect and punish this class of offenders, in consequence of a great number of gas lamps and windows having been broken in different parts of the borough. Amongst other offences referred to in the local acts; it is enacted that "every person who wantonly discharges any firearm, or throws or discharges any stone or other missile, or makes any bonfire, or throws or sets fire to any firework, to the danger or annoyance of residents or passengers, is liable to a penalty not exceeding forty shillings." Latterly I have had to proceed against several youths for discharging firearms and fireworks in the public streets or adjacent thereto, and penalties have been inflicted by the magistrates as a caution to others.'

- 33 people proceeded against for wilful damage.

- 39 cases of hawking without authority.

- 12 cases of neglect of work.

- Thirty-four persons arrested for begging. For other offences against the Vagrant Act 149 persons were dealt with.

- 'No case of canine madness has been reported to the police this year, therefore no notice has been issued for the confinement of dogs.'

- 344 pedlars' certificates were issued by the police.

- 'In January last the Chimney Sweepers Act came into force, and under that statue 28 certificates have been issued to chimney sweepers, authorising them to carry on their business in the borough.'

A member of the constabulary on the beat.

- 644 dwelling-house or warehouse doors and windows were found open or insecure by the police during the year.

- 438 public-houses, beerhouses, and shops held licences. Five publicans were dealt for offences against the law, two were convicted and three cases dismissed. During the same period nine beer sellers were summoned before the magistrates, four of whom were fined and five dismissed. Twelve felonies were reported to the police as having been committed in public-houses, and eleven from beerhouses.

- 1201 letters were written and dispatched from this office.

- 110 inquests were held by the Borough Coroner.

- 41 music licenses granted by the magistrates.

- '15 offences for which the drivers of hackney carriages have been prosecuted, including those proceeded against for drunkenness. One driver's license has been revoked.'

- 'The Gunpowder and Explosives Act came into force this year, under which nineteen applications for registration have been made to sell gunpowder and 'mixed explosives,' fifty-six for 'mixed explosives', only, and one room has been registered for the filling of cartridges for small arms. One shilling each is charged for registration, which has now to be done annually. Previous to the above Act coming into force a fee of 5s. was charged for a license, which was permanent. '

- 'There were dealers in petroleum under certain strength, and one person licensed to keep petroleum. 'Two persons have been fined during the year for keeping above a certain quantity of petroleum without having a license to do so.'

- £360 16s 3d received by the police during the year from the pedlars' certificates, endorsements, &c.

- 'The number of convicts in the borough who hold licenses or whose licenses have expired is 51, viz, 40 males and 11 females. There are also 10 males and 14 females under police supervision in the borough. Two males and two females of those under surveillance are required to report themselves to the police on their discharge from prison, or on removing from one police district to another, or on changing their residence. Two males have been imprisoned during the year and not reporting themselves on removing from one police district to Bolton.'

● 'On the 13th March last Captain Elgee, her Majesty's inspector of Constabulary, made his annual inspection of the police force, and also minutely examined the books and forms kept in the offices, and from the tenor of his remarks I have reason to believe that the force has been maintained in a state of efficiency. A change of material, &c., for the police capes was recommended by the inspector, and adopted in September of this year.'

● 'Two deaths have occurred in the force during the year – viz, those of P. S. Whittle and P. C. Crossley. The average number of day's sickness in the force per annum is 1,070 and the daily average 293. The police superannuated fund now amounts to £5,155 4s 11d against £4,867 15s. 6d. last year. The sum of £386 11s. 4d. has been paid during the year just ended to superannuated police-officers and constables, and to the widows of the deceased members of the force. Last year the amount expended for these purposes was £350 16s 10d.'

● The cost of the police force (consisting of 100 officers and constables) in pay and clothing was £8529; 'one-half of which is paid by Government'. In 1867 the number of police was forty, and the cost to the borough was then £3,051.

BOLTON TABLES OF CRIME

Degree of education of those persons charged with felony during 1875 and 1876:

PERSONS				
1875	WELL	IMPERFECT	NONE	TOTAL
ADULTS	18	138	77	233
JUVENILES	-	29	21	50
TOTAL	18	167	98	283

PERSONS				
1876	WELL	IMPERFECT	NONE	TOTAL
ADULTS	22	162	117	304
JUVENILES	-	16	13	29
TOTAL	22	178	130	330

Number of cases brought before the magistrates in each year under the Elementary Act since the formation of the School Board:

1871-2		1872-3		1873-4		1874-5		1875-6	
M	F	M	F	M	F	M	F	M	F
45	9	158	30	307	51	471	81	279	66

Number of persons proceeded against in the several police districts in Lancashire during the year ended 30 June 30th for the offences therein to:-

District	Assaulting the Police	All Other Assaults	Breach Of The Peace	Disorderly Prostitutes	Total
Ashton	34	96	21	6	157
Blackburn	71	8-2	16	21	910
Bolton	84	374	9-6	115	1539
Lancaster	11	40	12	0	63
Liverpool	1071	1584	486	3864	6988
Manchester	612	2570	1208	1391	5786
Oldham	52	443	96	18	6-4
Preston	64	327	130	2	523
Rochdale	59	394	-4	8	525
Salford	221	512	144	64	941
Southport	11	104	19	10	144
Stalybridge	15	86	176	0	277
Warrington	40	245	175	3	463
Wigan	41	135	86	8	270
Count/Police Districts	614	5399	2099	79	8182
TOTAL	3000	13,102	5878	5585	27,365

Number and cost of the conveyance of prisoners during the last ten years:

| | COST OF CONVEYANCE | | | NO. CONVEYED TO PRISON |
	£	s.	d.	
1867	46	19	4	516
1868	58	6	1	671
1869	62	6	0	743
1870	18	14	8	807
1871	67	12	3	729
1872	68	10	10	721
1873	79	7	10	855
1874	93	19	6	1078
1875	105	0	11	1133
1876	111	5	1	1224

Number of communications issued in four years as follows:

YEAR	LETTERS	ROUTES	OTHER COMMUNITIES	TOTAL
1870-71	674	274	-	948
1872-73	768	381	-	1149
1874-75	800	617	-	1417
1875-76	1201	936	891	3028
TOTAL	1443	2208	891	6542

Number of days the police have been absent on the sick list during four years ending 29 September 1876:

MONTH	1872-3 NO. OF DAYS	1873-4 NO. OF DAYS	1874-5 NO.OF DAYS	1875-6 NO. OF DAYS
OCTOBER	93	81	124	91
NOVEMBER	50	94	123	135
DECEMBER	68	131	163	123
JANUARY	3-	10-	190	98
FEBRUARY	57	94	93	135
MARCH	75	91	94	73
APRIL	79	124	85	114
MAY	12	74	63	155
JUNE	17	40	130	140
JULY	19	47	92	82
AUGUST	40	84	102	97
SEPTEMBER	25	96	72	81
TOTALS	571	1056	3331	1324
STRENGTH OF THE FORCE IN EACH YEAR	97	97	98	100
DAYS AVERAGE SICKNESS	156	289	365	363

Deansgate, *c.* 1880. (Image courtesy of Chris Driver)

ONE

AARON MELLOR
– THE BOLTON MURDER, 1857

(FROM THE *BOLTON JOURNAL*, 12 DECEMBER 1857)

(By our own reporter)

His lordship took his seat at ten o'clock.

THE BOLTON MURDER.

Aaron Mellor, 33, besom maker, was charged, on the coroner's inquisition, for that he did, at Bolton, on the 1st October last, 'feloniously, wilfully, and of his malice aforethought,' kill and murder Alice Mellor, his wife. Mr. Sowler and Mr. Higgin (instructed by Mr. Gaskell, public prosecutor for this borough) prosecuted; and Mr. J. H. Fernley (instructed by Mr. H. M. Richardson, solicitor, of this town) defended. The prisoner looked remarkably well, and in a firm tone he pleaded, 'Not Guilty.' The only Bolton person on the jury was Mr. Daniel Brown, manufacturer, and he, having been challenged by the counsel for the defence, was obliged to retire. The court was densely crowded with spectators.

Mr. Sowler, in opening the case, said the prisoner was charged with the wilful murder of his wife, and the circumstances under which that took place he would narrate to them very briefly, and without any comments at all. He should leave the matter entirely in the hands of the jury, after having laid before them a short sketch of the evidence. It seemed that about five years before this fatal affair took place, the prisoner and the deceased were married; and the living offspring of that marriage consisted of three children, the eldest of which was about four years of age. It seemed further that from the very time of their marriage, prisoner and deceased lived very unhappily together, so much so, that finding they could no longer live together, on the 26th September last the deceased left his house and went to sleep at the house of a man named Cunningham, taking her meals at her mother's. Now, between seven and eight o'clock on the evening of the 1st October, the deceased was getting her supper in her mother's house, with her mother, when the prisoner went in, rather the worse for drink. It seemed some conversation took place between the prisoner and deceased in reference to her returning to his house. She refused to go home, alleging that there was nothing to go to, but a damp cellar in which there had been no fire for a week, and that she had her children, if they did return, would take their deaths of cold. A proposition was then made, by the deceased, he believed, that she should take another of the children, a boy named Tom (she had then with her a baby seven months old), and she said to the prisoner, if he could not manage to keep the one remaining, she would endeavour to take and keep that also, and then he might have his free liberty. Upon this, the prisoner left the house: put his hand upon the deceased's shoulder and said he wanted her to let him clip her, adding that he would not hurt a hair on her head. He then went out again, and in a few minutes afterwards, deceased and her mother went out, the mother for the purpose of purchasing some bread for the children, and the deceased to go to her lodgings. They went down Crown Street, and had got very near the bridge when they heard the prisoner running after them. They turned round and went towards him. Something passed between prisoner and deceased. Prisoner asked her again if she would go home, and this time it appeared she said she would. However, some conversion took place between the mother-in-law and the prisoner, and the prisoner told her she had better go away, or she would be sorry. Upon this, the old woman crossed over to the opposite side of the street, and the prisoner and deceased continued to walk up the street together towards Deansgate, evidently not on amicable terms, for words were passing between them. It seemed that when they got at the corner of Crown Street, opposite Mr. Plimmer's shoe shop, prisoner gave his wife a shove, and then said 'What are you for, what are you about?' They then crossed the street, and here, opposite the shop of Mr. Scowcroft, druggist, the prisoner's foot caught in a ring in the gutter used for the purpose of letting casks into the cellar, and he stumbled, but did not fall. They appeared still to be having words. They then crossed to the other side of Deansgate, opposite Mr. Blake's spirit vaults, and there some more conversation took place between prisoner and deceased. At length, a person of the name of Hampson would tell the jury that he saw the prisoner run up to deceased and begin to strike her very violently about the head, that then the prisoner threw his arm round her neck, put his hand down the side of his trowsers, and drew forth a large knife, with which he commenced cutting at her throat; and no sooner had prisoner cut his wife's throat then he cut his own, and the knife – a most formidable instrument, as the jury would see when it was produced – dropped from his hand. Both prisoner and deceased were conveyed to the Infirmary; the deceased was dead when they got her there, and it would appear from the testimony of the surgeon that death must have been almost instantaneous. The prisoner was confined at the Infirmary for a considerable time, the wound inflicted upon his own throat by himself being such as to place his life in peril. From the surgeon's testimony, there must have been three distinct cuts to produce the ghastly wounds in the deceased's throat: in fact, her head was nearly cut off. The knife would be laid before the jury; it was one used by the prisoner in his trade as a besom maker; to trim twigs, and wounds inflicted upon the deceased were of such a character as this knife might have produced. The surgeon would tell them that between the second and third vertebrae, what he described as the third wound, and that it must have been with very considerable violence, inasmuch as the knife had penetrated to the spinal marrow, and therefore death would ensue almost instantly. He told them just now, prisoner and deceased had lived very unhappily together. A piece of evidence had transpired since the coroner's inquest, a copy of which had been handed to the counsel for the defence. [Mr. Fernley: Only yesterday.] But Mr. Fernley was told this additional evidence would be received, on Saturday last. That evidence might or might not be important. It might be important, inasmuch as it would show, more distinctly than anything else could, the shocking terms upon which the prisoner and the deceased lived together. The police-constable George Sharples would tell them that some four or five months before this occurrence, he happened to be passing the prisoner's house and that the deceased came running out screaming.

Mr. Fernley rose to make an objection to this additional evidence, when his Lordship observed that Mr. Sowler had better not allude to it further, and that Mr. Fernley might object to it when it came to be offered by the witness.

Mr. Sowler: Then, gentleman, the case stands as I have represented it to you. A witness will be called who will tell you that he had been drinking with the prisoner at Halliwell on this day of the alleged murder, he will tell you at that time the prisoner had the knife, as he was constantly in the habit of carrying it in the left-hand pocket of his sleeve-waistcoat. You must deal with this evidence, gentleman, as I have no doubt you will, with fairness both towards the Crown and the prisoner. If you can see any possibility, under his Lordship's direction, of reducing the crime to that of manslaughter, I am sure, under that direction, you will only be too happy to do so. If, on the other hand, the facts do not warrant you in reducing the offence, and are such as to leave you no alternative but to find the prisoner guilty of the crime of murder which is now imputed to him, you must do your duty, and leave hereafter others to do theirs, if it be necessary to make any alternation in the fate which overhangs this man.

The following evidence was then called for the prosecution: Ann Mulloy, mother of the deceased (examined by Mr. Higgin): I am a widow, residing in Back Crown Street, Bolton. My daughter was married to the prisoner. (Here the witness looked towards the prisoner, and almost immediately fainted. She was carried out of the court by two officers, and the occurrence seemed to produce much sensation amongst the spectators.)

Mr. Fernley: As most of the facts will be admitted, I should not have pressed with witness much.

It was then agreed to call the other evidence first.

William Hampson: I am a porter in the employment of Mr. Scowcroft, druggist, Bolton, whose shop fronts Deansgate and Crown Street. I remember the night of the 1st of October. About ten minutes before eight that night I was in a passage that leads from Crown Street to Back Crown Street. I saw a man and two women talking together. The prisoner is the man. I heard him say to the old woman, the mother of the deceased, 'Go home, or else you'll be sorry.' The old woman then went in the direction of Back Crown Street, and the prisoner and the other woman went towards Deansgate. Whilst they were going up Crown Street, I heard them grumbling and falling out. When near Mr. Plimmer's shoe shop, at the corner of

Crown Street, I saw the prisoner clap (place) his hand on the deceased's shoulder, and she turned round and said 'What are you for?' That was all that passed there. They then went on a bit further into Deansgate, opposite Mr. Scowcroft's shop, and then he clapped his hand on her shoulder again, and offered to strike her, but he did not strike her. She then turned round and gave him a shove with her elbow, and then he made a kind of a stumble in a ring in the pavement used to let casks into the cellar; but he did not fall. They then went on a bit further, having more words; but I did not quite catch what was said. They went across Deansgate, and had some words there, and then they went on the footpath opposite Mr. Blake's vaults. They had some more words on the footpath. I could hear them chunnering (grumbling), but could not tell what she said. Then he made a bit of a struggle at her, and stuck her three or four times. They went about a yard further after that, and I saw him rush at her again, then strike her again; and then they went to the door. I heard her scream 'Murder', and I ran towards them. When I got there two men were pulling him off her, and I caught hold of the prisoner's right shoulder and pulled him up. Then he went on the floor on his back, and I saw his throat was cut. I did not see what state the deceased was in. Both were taken to the Infirmary.

Cross-examined by Mr. Fernley: We had to support the prisoner. His throat was cut, and he was bleeding very extensively. The distance from Mr. Scowcroft's shop to Mr. Blake's vaults may be 20 yards, and from Mr. Plimmer's shop 28 or 30 yards; but I cannot say exactly. Deansgate is a street very much frequented. Many thousands of people pass it every day. It is one of the most crowded streets in the town, and people are passing all hours of the day. There is a dark passage near Mr. Blake's vaults, which leads from Deansgate to the Shambles. It is not well lighted, and any one going down there might do so without being seen. Prisoner and deceased might have gone up there, and then they would not have been seen. This passage is about two yards from the place where this occurrence happened. I had seen the prisoner before. I am not aware that his head has been very much bruised. I never spoke to the man in my life. I never examined his head, and cannot tell whether it presents marks of considerable violence.

Edward Duckworth: I am a cabinet maker. I was in Deansgate, in Bolton, on Thursday night, the 1st October, about ten minutes to eight o'clock. I was standing opposite Mr. Chaplin's carpet shop. I saw the prisoner. There was a woman with him, and she a child in her arms. They were standing opposite Chaplin's. She said something to him that she would do when she got home, but I did not hear what it was. He said, 'Will you?' She replied, 'Yes, I will.' He then struck her. Then she was falling, and he put his arm around her neck. He then drew a knife out, and drew it across her throat. He drew it from somewhere about the right side of his leg. She screamed out just as she was falling, and they both dropped to the ground together. I saw the prisoner use the knife while he was down. He used it on her neck while she was on the ground. I got up to them as soon as I could, and pulled him off, and then he pulled the knife across his own throat, after which he placed it on the ground by his right leg. Some other person took away the knife.

Cross-examined by Mr. Fernley: The prisoner looked very wild. He might know what he was doing, but he had had some drink. I did not see them before they got opposite Chaplin's. I am certain prisoner did not pull his arm round deceased's waist. They were quarrelling together, and went off towards Blake's vaults, which is about ten yards from the place I first saw them. There was a bit of a struggle by the vaults.

By his Lordship: the struggle was when he was cutting her – when he was doing the deed.

By Mr. Fernley: I did not see her shove him into the street, nor anything of that kind. He bled very hard after cutting his own throat. I don't know whether, three or four years since, he was very much beaten about the head. I never heard any complaints from him about his head. I have not examined his head. I have never examined anything about him.

John Stathers: I was in Deansgate on Thursday evening the 1st October, about five or ten minutes to eight. I heard a scream from the direction of the Old Shambles, close to Blake's vaults. I went there and saw the deceased. She was laid across the causeway. I saw the prisoner also laid down on his back, and two men holding him. I picked up the knife from the side of his right leg and gave it Sergeant Grime.

A policeman in early uniform.

Sergeant Grime, of the Bolton police force, produced the knife, which was still besmeared with blood.

Mr. Fernley: It is the knife which I believe the prisoner used in cutting ling. Ling grows in the neighbourhood of Halliwell.

Police-constable George Sharples: I was on duty in Deansgate on the night of Thursday, the 1st October. I heard scream of 'Murder,' and I went towards Blake's vaults, in which direction the scream had proceeded. On arriving there I saw the deceased. She was in a leaning position. Some parties had hold of her. She was bleeding very much from the right side of her head. I saw the prisoner there also, and on his right side was a knife. I took him into the Red Lion public-house, close by, and then I found that his throat was cut. I then took him to the Infirmary.

The question of the additional evidence to be given by this witness was here raised, and his Lordship said he thought it had better not be offered, for it seemed to him the value of it was not great.

Mr. Sowler expressed his concurrence in the view of his Lordship, and it was accordingly not offered.

John Garrett: I am a tinker, I have known the prisoner for several years. On Thursday morning the 1st October he was in my cellar. He and I had a good deal to drink together at Halliwell during the day. The knife produced is the knife he got his living with. He had it in his waistcoat pocket, on the left side. It was a sleeve waistcoat.

Cross-examined by Mr. Fernley: Halliwell is about two miles from Bolton, a portion of it; it is a little higher up where the brooms grow. The prisoner carried out the knife about with him for the purpose of getting besom wood. I have seen his head. (Here prisoner exhibited the back of his head. He got into a row and was kicked very badly). (Prisoner again showed the back of his head, but pointed to another part of it). He showed me that as having been kicked there also. I did not witness the kicking. His head was badly bruised. His face was terribly bruised. He was very strange that day, very shocking. He really did not know what he was doing that day, for he even said to me, 'if the devil had got hold of him, he would be in hell before morning'; so I will leave you to guess that state of mind he was in. Before he got these kicks, he was more rational, and quite a different sort of man. He could not wash his face for the bruises, and after that I noticed these peculiarities. After his wife and he parted, he was quite deranged. He had got beaten on the Saturday morning previous to parting from his wife, and his head and face was bruised. That was the Saturday before this matter happened.

I saw him every day after receiving these injuries. He appeared different, quite in a deranged state. I was very frightened of him. He did go about his trade as usual.

By his Lordship: He could not exactly go about his trade as usual, because he was left with these two children. His wife left him on the Saturday before this Thursday night. When he was not looking after the children, he did go to his work.

Re-examined by Mr. Sowler: I was not with him when he got the bruises. It is only from what I heard, but I saw the injuries every day.

By the jury: All the bruises were received on the Saturday, as I understand.

Mr. John Segar, M.D., house surgeon at the Bolton Infirmary, said he saw the deceased a minute or two after being brought into the Infirmary, on the night of the 1st October. She was quite dead. He afterwards examined her head and neck. There was a large wound extending from near the left ear and across the back of the neck to the right side of the mouth, and half separating the head from the body. He attributed her death to that wound. The opinion he formed at the post mortem examination was that the wound had been made by three cuts. The instrument, whether it was by which they had been inflicted, had penetrated the spinal marrow. The knife produced was such an instrument as the wounds might have been inflicted. The cuts were not in a direct line. Apparently three incisions had been made with the knife, but all formed one large wound.

Ann Mulloy was then examined. She appeared to be in a very nervous state, and as she stood, in the witness box she rested on her right elbow and held her handkerchief to the side of her face as if to avoid seeing the prisoner. Mr. Fernley, seeing her state, proposed to admit everything she had to say, but his Lordship said she had better be examined. The witness then deposed to the following effect:- My daughter and the prisoner lived in Velvet-walks. I remember her going to Daniel Cunningham's. She had her meals with me then. On the night of the 1st October, she was at my house. She had her child in her arms. The prisoner came while she was there, and sat on a slopstone beside the door. After he had been in a short time, he said to his wife, 'How long have you a mind to stop here?' 'Till you fetch me out of it,' she said. 'Will you come now – will you come to-night?' he asked. She replied, 'I have no home to come to but a cold cellar, that has had no fire in since I left; but I will take Tom (that was the second child) and then you may keep the other, or I'll take both if you like.' He said, 'Will you come and take him to-night?' 'No,' she said, 'not while morning.' He then went out for a few minutes. When he came back, he closed the door after him. He then came and dropped on one knee on front of where she was sitting, put up his left arm towards her neck, and said

'Clip me, wench, you know I wouldn't hurt a hair on your head.' She left the child down by her knee and pushed him away, saying, 'You have a knife about you, you knew; and I know you of old.' (Sensation.) He got up then off his knee, and asked her, 'Would she take the child that night?' She said 'No; in the morning.' He said 'It's right.' I then took the child up in my arms, and he asked me to shake hands. I said 'it was out of fashion.' He then bade me good night, and went away. She turned and finished her supper, which she was eating when he came in the first time. We made no great delay, but prepared to go to where she lodged. We went out together, she with the child in her arms. We had got nearly as far as the bridge in Crown Street, which is a lonesome part, when I heard him coming running after us. We turned back to meet him. He asked where we were going. I said, 'To get some bread for the children's supper.' He said, 'Never mind the children they are right enough.' He and his wife went both on one side, and I kept in the middle of the street for a few yards. I heard him ask her would she come home, and she said 'Yes,' and that was the last word I heard

my child speak. He turned round to me then, and said, 'I'm none married to you; do you go back.' 'I know you are not,' I said, 'but I'll do no harm; I'm just going up here to get some bread for the children's supper.' He again said. 'Never mind the children, they're right enough.' I said they could not be right enough when he was off fuddling. After they had gone a short distance further, he turned back to me again and said, 'Go back, or you'll be sorry.' 'God bless us, I will,' said I, so I turned as if to go into Back Crown Street, and walked on the other side, so that he could not see me.

Cross-examining a key witness…

They went on talking together, and when I got to the top of Crown Street they were at the other side of Deansgate. I looked across and was terrified. I thought I saw him raise his arm. I rushed to them. First I saw him lying on his back, and I heard them saying he had cut her throat, and that she was dead, for he had cut her head nearly off. I can tell no more.

Mr. Fernley: I do not ask her anything.

Mr. Sowler intimated that this was the case for the prosecution. After an interval of ten minutes for refreshments, Mr. Fernley rose to address the jury for the defence. He assured them that he had entered into the case, supported only by the hope that they would, as far as they could, coincide with the views which he should venture to suggest to them. He must admit that their verdict must be, at all events, one of manslaughter; and he did most sincerely hope that when they had heard the few remarks which he should make, they would say this was not a case in which they would return a verdict of wilful murder. He did not know whether it had ever happened to them, but it had always struck him that the appearance of a court of justice on a trial for murder, of itself conveyed a most salutary lesson. Though he had defended a great number of prisoners in his short career, he never ventured on a case in which he felt as much as the present, because he felt that each hour which passed was bringing this poor man (if they found a verdict of wilful murder) nearer to the scaffold, nearer to the grave. The prisoner was indicted for wilful murder. Murder was a crime committed in secret. It was a crime on which, usually, no human eyes ever looked. It was one of those crimes which, at all events if premeditated, often baffle the energies of the best officers, and very often indeed the murderers evaded justice. In this case there was nothing of the kind. If they believed this to be a murder, it was certainly a most extraordinary one. He could not deny it was done by the prisoner, but it was committed in the greatest thoroughfare of Bolton, in the presence of a great number of individuals, some of whom had come to testify against him. The prisoner did it apparently without the least motive, without any of that malice which the law imputed in the case of wilful murder. Malice might be of two kinds, either express or implied. Express malice would be where a person placed himself in ambush and coolly awaited the approach of his unsuspecting victim. Implied malice was that which the law presumed from an act of violence committed without reasonable motive. The jury had one case before them a short time since, the result of which they all knew; and he sincerely hoped that in this case the result might be the same. In this case, there had been some trifling disagreement between the prisoner and deceased, and as often took place between husband and wife; but there was no pretence for saying that up to that time he bore any ill-feeling towards her. As far as they knew, she was a woman whom he admired, loved, and reverenced; and although there might, as he had said, have been some trifling disagreement, yet it was by no means of that character to support a motive such as which the prosecution would import. According to the evidence, the prisoner had sustained a severe injury to the head and face on the previous Saturday; so brutal, indeed, had the attack been, that his face was disfigured till he could not wash it. On the Thursday after this, he discovered the whereabouts of his wife – that she was taking her meals at her mother's house, and lodging at the house of a person called Cunningham; and it was evident that he laid no ill feeling against her at this time, for he said, 'When will you come back? Will you come now?' She refused at the moment, and he left the house, but immediately returned, and if ever repentance was shown it was in this man's act for on bended knee to his wife he said, 'Come with me now, and let me clip you, and I will never hurt a hair on your head.' She received him in the same spirit, went out with him and consented to return home with him, and then all at once some quarrel arose, and in a moment of excitement, perhaps in consequence of what his wife had said to him, he committed the fatal deed. (Here the learned counsel appeared to be much affected, and the prisoner also buried his face in his hands and wept bitterly.) There was (continued Mr. Fernley) no premeditation; the prisoner, foolishly enough, had been drinking in Halliwell; maddened by habitual drinking, and in consequence of the personal injuries he had sustained on the previous Saturday, he went to his wife; a quarrel arose, but what she said during that quarrel would never be known. The knife with which the offence was committed the prisoner always carried about with him for the purpose of his trade, as a joiner did his rule, and he might therefore have used it in the impulse of the moment; and there was no telling what provocation he might have received at the hands of the deceased. It was clear she used some violence, for one of the witnesses spoke to seeing her give the prisoner a shove, and if she used expressions with it calculated to excite him still further, he (Mr. Fernley) was quite sure the jury, making due allowance for human frailty, would not find this man guilty of wilful murder. Besides, the wound of which this poor woman died was not inflicted, as they usually found in cases of murder, upon the throat, but upon the back of the neck, the prisoner having the knife in his right hand, and he mentioned this as some ground for supposing that the prisoner did not intend to take her life.

Under the direction of his Lordship, Dr. Segar was here recalled, in consequence of some misapprehension as to the nature of the wound. He described the wound as commencing about an inch from the left ear, extending round the back of the neck and ending at the mouth. There was no wound in front.

Mr. Fernley resumed his address. He laid great stress upon the circumstances under which the offence was committed, and contended that all tended to prove that it was done without any premeditation, and under the influence of passion brought on by the attacks of his wife, and aggravated by drink and by the injuries to his head which he had received on the previous Saturday. Had the prisoner premeditated the murder of his wife, he would not have perpetrated it in the most public thoroughfare in Bolton, but would rather have lured her into the dark passage near the spot, where he could have done it unnoticed. And having committed it he made no attempt to escape, but such was his frenzied state that he cut his own throat, and it was only by the exercise of great skill on the part of the medical men that his life was saved. He urged, in conclusion, that it was one of those cases in which the evidence on the part of the prosecution had failed; and he hoped that, considering the injuries which the prisoner had sustained to his head, and the way in which he conducted himself after those injuries, there was sufficient to induce the jury to return a verdict of manslaughter, and not of wilful murder.

His Lordship summed up the evidence. He observed the prisoner was indicted for murder of his wife, and undoubtedly the injury was one of the most serious – it might be one of the most painful – in which a jury could be placed. On the one hand, if they were satisfied beyond all reasonable doubt that that which the law defined to be murder had occurred in this case – he need not remark to them it would be their bounden duty to find a verdict against the prisoner the benefit of any reasonable doubt. If they entertained such doubt in this case, they must acquit the prisoner of the higher offence, for public justice required it. The question for their consideration, then, was whether in this case those circumstances did occur which constituted the offence of wilful murder, or whether there were those circumstances which reduced it to manslaughter. It was not a question whether or not the prisoner was a responsible agent, because the learned counsel for the prisoner had hardly raised that question; for unless the prisoner was so devoid of reason as to be incapable of distinguishing between right and wrong, he must be answerable for the consequences of his act. In point of law, the killing of a person was presumed to be murder in the first instance, unless there were other circumstances in the case which showed the absence of the malicious intent to kill or do grievous bodily harm which was the essence of the crime of murder. Now, he was bound to tell the jury also that it was not every slight provocation – by a 'shove,' for example – that would justify the use of such an instrument as a knife in such a manner as to cause death. Indeed, the consequences would be most dangerous to society if such were the case; if mere language, if the slightest touch upon the person were considered a sufficient provocation to justify the infliction of death. The law was not so. In order to reduce homicide below the crime of murder, it must appear that there were such reasonable provocation and such circumstances as the law, paying some regard to the infirmity of human feeling, would consider a palliation, something that would show that the person committing the offence was acting upon some sudden passion, arising from the violence inflicted. In the present case, there certainly did not seem to have been any provocation beyond that shove. Now, as to the injuries spoken to by the tinker Garrett as having been received by the prisoner on the Saturday before the murder. It did not appear that those injuries were of such a kind as to prevent him attending to his work. It did not appear either, that he had any medical attendance, nor did there seem to have been any such injury received as would warrant the conclusion that on account of those injuries the prisoner was devoid of understanding, and labouring under such aberration of intellect as not to be able to distinguish right from wrong. But, it was said he did it in the time of great excitement. No doubt that might be so. He might have been in a state of very considerable excitement; but it would be highly dangerous to society if men, giving away to such excited feelings, were induced to take away the life of those who had caused that excitement. That undoubtedly would be the crime of wilful murder. Then the question was, did the prisoner receive such provocation – such reasonable provocation – as would reduce this crime to that of manslaughter?

… It was however, for the jury to consider whether at the time he did it the prisoner did act under a feeling a provocation such as would warrant the infliction of such a wound. If there was reasonable provocation, their verdict must be manslaughter; but if they believed he committed the offence from mere passion, and without reasonable and sufficient ground of provocation, then, however painful it might be, it would be their duty to find the prisoner guilty of wilful murder.

The jury then retired to consider their verdict, and after an absence from court of from a quarter of an hour to twenty minutes, retuned a verdict of 'Guilty of wilful murder'.

A row of cells.

The Judge then assumed the black cap, and in the most solemn and impressive manner proceeded to pass sentence of death upon the prisoner. Addressing him, his Lordship said:- Aaron Mellor, the jury, after a careful consideration of your case, have come to the conclusion – and I am sure they must have had no other course – that you are guilty of the crime with which you were charged, wilful murder; and I believe that all who have heard this distressing case must feel satisfied that under the circumstances of this case, you have been rightly judged. From some feelings of irritation, arising from the fact of your wife having left you, you were induced to commit this dreadful act which deprived her of life. There is no reasonable ground for believing that at that time you were so devoid of reason as to be incapable of distinguishing between right and wrong, so as to render you an irresponsible agent; and though your counsel has, in the exercise of his direction, pressed that point, it is not warranted by the evidence. Your counsel has urged all that he possibly could on your behalf, but there is no evidence in your case to show that there was any adequate provocation which might have amounted, not a justification, but to a mitigation, of the crime from the dreadful one of murder. I am unwilling to aggravate your feelings by any remarks to mine; but let me earnestly entreat you to make the most of the time that is allotted to you, for I have no authority to hold out hopes of mercy; and I hope and entreat that you will endeavour by earnest prayer.

The prisoner (in a loud distinct voice): My lord judge, I'm a murdered man.

His Lordship continued: The sentence upon you is that you to be taken to the place from whence you came, that you thence conveyed to the place of execution, and there be hanged by the neck until you are dead, and that your body be buried within the precincts of the gaol within which you have last been confirmed; and may the Lord have mercy upon your soul.

The prisoner was then removed from the dock without evincing the slightest emotion, but on turning round to descend to the cell, he raised his eyes above the level of the dock, glanced hastily round, and recognising some one in the body of the court, he waved his hand as if bidding a last adieu. A person in front of the spectators replied in the same way, and he then hastily but firmly descended the steps. The case lasted nearly three hours.

Defrauding the Bolton Corporation, 1872

(FROM THE *BOLTON JOURNAL* 17 FEBRUARY 1872)

ARTHUR WHITTAKER, INSPECTOR OF PAVIORS

On Thursday, at the Borough Court, a young man, named Arthur Whittaker, inspector of paviors, Belfast, Ireland, late of Bolton, was charged with obtaining, by false pretences, from John Tonge, the sum of 19s., as wages due to John France, on the 27th January last, with intent to defraud the Mayor, Alderman and Burgesses of the Borough of Bolton.

Mr. Rutter (Messer. Hall and Rutter) prosecuted, and opened the case by detailing the circumstances under which the charge was laid. He then proceeded to call evidence. James Harper, bookkeeper in the Surveyor's Department of the Bolton Corporation, said it was part of his duty to keep a book called 'The Street Wages Book', which he produced. In that book was entered the names of the workmen engaged under the Street Committee, and the wages due to each of them. The particulars in that book were entered from small pocket books kept by the different inspectors. Prisoner was in the employ of the Bolton Corporation, and on the 19th January the prisoner handed in a book containing the names of the men who worked under him. From that book witness entered the names into the Streets Wages Book. On Wednesday, the 24th January, prisoner gives him, in

The Charge Desk.

the usual course, the names and time of the men including those of James Wilson and James France. The amount of wages stated to be to due to James Wilson up the Thursday night was 19s., and a similar sum to James France for a full week's work as labourers. After the book was made up by witness, it was taken to the treasurer's office.

John Tonge, clerk in the treasurer's department, said it was part of his duty to pay the workmen in the employ of the Bolton Corporation, and for that purpose he received a book from the Surveyor's Office, stating the amount due to each man. The wages were paid on the Friday night. On the 26th January witness paid the wages in the usual way. He called out the names of each man, and as he did so they stepped forward for their wages. When James Wilson's name was called, William Hall came forward, and when he did so prisoner said it would be all right. Witness paid Hall 19s. On calling out the name of John France no one answered, but prisoner was present. He retained France's wages, 19s., and prisoner came the following morning to the office, and received the amount. Witness asked how it was that France could not come himself, and prisoner replied that he was working at Burden or Rose Hill, it would be too far for him to come in order to get to the office in time.

James Seddon, inspector in the Sewering Department of the Bolton Corporation, said on Tuesday, the 30th January, he made inquires of all the men and could not ascertain that there were any men employed as labourers under the Corporation named either James Wilson or John France, though there were two men named John France employed as stonemasons. William Hall, a labourer in the employ of the Bolton Corporation, said he was working in Churchgate, during the whole of the week ending the 25th January. He had since ascertained the names of all the men employed there during that time, but there were none named James Wilson or John France. The 26th January was pay day, and witness ceased working at 5.20 in the evening. On his way to the Corporation Offices for the purpose of receiving his wage, prisoner met him at the corner of Princess Street and said, he wanted witness to draw Wilson's wages, remarking at the same time that he 'liked' to have forgotten all about it.

Witness consented to do as he was asked. He inquired how much the amount was, and prisoner said '19s. a full week's wages.' Witness did not know Wilson, and asked prisoner who he was. Prisoner replied that he was one of the odd men, and said witness was to give the 19s. to him (prisoner). Witness went to the treasurer's office for the purpose of receiving his wages. He heard the name of James Wilson called, and stepped forward for the money. Prisoner, who was standing by at the time, said the man had gone to a funeral. Witness received the 19s. and then went to the corner of the Market Square, when he waited till the prisoner came, and gave him the 19s. Prisoner did not give him anything for doing so.

John Harley, labourer, in the employ of the Bolton Corporation, said he was engaged at St. George's Yard. He worked there every day up to the 25th January. There were no men named James Wilson and John France employed there.

Thomas Ainscow yardman at the Wellington yard, gave evidence that no men of the names of James Wilson or John France were employed at that yard.

Churchgate, *c.* 1901.

Richard Booth, paviour, in the employ of the Bolton Corporation, said he worked under the prisoner in Churchgate, along with other men, on the 19th, 20th and 25th January last. There were no men working there on those dates named either James Wilson or John France.

Detective-Sergt Greenhalgh deposed to receiving the prisoner into custody from the police at Belfast, on Monday last. Witness charged the prisoner the same day at Belfast, and he replied, 'I am very sorry; what there is wrong I will work for and make it right again.'

The Judge's chair.

Prisoner pleaded guilty to the charge. He said he was exceedingly sorry for what had been done, and hoped the Bench would be lenient. The magistrates committed him for trail at the sessions.

(FROM THE *BOLTON JOURNAL*, 6 APRIL 1872)

TRIAL OF PRISONER
EMBEZZLEMENT BY A SERVANT OF THE CORPORATION

Arthur Whittaker 30, paviour, was indicted for having obtained by false pretences the sum of £3.16s. at various times, from John Tonge agent to the Mayor, Alderman and Burgesses of the Borough of Bolton. Prisoner pleaded guilty, and was defended by Mr. Blair. Prisoner was employed as foreman in the service of the Corporation, at the time he committed the offences he was charged with. For the defence, Mr. Blair admitted that the offence was a most serious one, because the prisoner held a responsible position. He had been out on bail since he was remanded, and the gentleman who had employed him, gave him an excellent character, saying that he had been perfectly honest during the time he had been in his employ. Prior to committing the offence, he had also borne an exceptionally good character. Prisoner was committed to six months imprisonment.

A model of a prisoner in the cells awaiting trial.

THREE

A Child Murder in Bolton, 1876

(FROM THE *JOURNAL*, SATURDAY 1 JANUARY 1876)

On Wednesday, John Taylor, Esq., Borough Coroner, held an inquest on the body of a newly-born female child, which was found on the footpath in St. George's Road opposite the Temperance Hall on Christmas Eve.

Mr. Edward Sergeant, medical officer of health, said he made a post-mortem examination of the body on the 28th inst. He found the body fairly developed but small. It was probably a nine months child. On the right forearm there was a slight discolouration and swelling, which appeared to have been caused whilst there was vitality in the body. The skin over the abdomen was also slightly discoloured, but he could not say whether that discolouration took place before or after birth, or during parturition. The internal organs were all healthy. The lungs had not been inflated with air, showing that the child had not had a separate existence.

John Smith said he was on St. George's Road on Friday night last, opposite the Temperance Hall. He saw a parcel lying on the footpath he picked it up, and put it under his coat. It contained the body of a child wrapped in two towels, and a sheet of brown paper. When he arrived at home he sent for a police officer, and delivered the body to him. The jury returned a verdict of 'Wilful Murder against some person unknown.'

We are requested to give the following description of the articles that were with the body of the child found on St. George's Road. It was wrapped in two hand towels and a piece of brown paper. The towel which was next to the body is a little marked with blood, is what is termed 'nap' or Russian' towelling, the size of which is 28in by 21in board, had a red stripe and tape like border at each end, about three quarters of an inch wide, and is very far worn. The second is known as 'honeycomb' or 'huckaback' towelling, about half worn, is 33in by 18.5in, it has four double stripes of red running from end to end, five inches apart, and a red stripe three quarters of an inch broad at each end, with fringe border, two very small holes at one end, and is quite clean, as if it had been recently taken from a drawer. These articles can now be inspected at the Police Office.

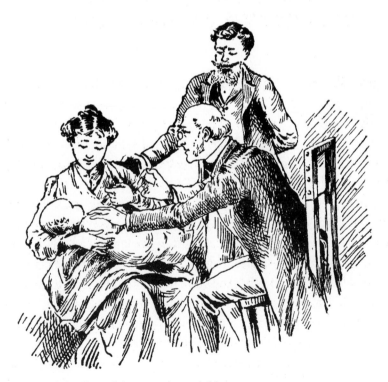

A Victorian family and their new-born child.

The Court.

FOUR

A BOLTON BROTHEL-KEEPER HEAVILY FINED

(FROM THE *BOLTON WEEKLY JOURNAL*, SATURDAY 2 FEBRUARY 1876)

At the Borough Court, on Thursday, Thomas Hunt, 15 Crown Entry, Deansgate, was charged with keeping a brothel on the 7th inst. Mr. Robinson defended. Police Sergeant Rhodes said that shortly after 12 o'clock at midnight on Sunday last, from information he received, he went to defendant's lodging house, and remained at the door for a short time, and looked through the keyhole and saw a man named Frederick Elliott, a coachman, and a women named Elizabeth Charleston, a ballet girl; the latter had a lighted candle in her hand. He heard them say 'good night,' and proceed upstairs into a room. At 25 minutes past 12, defendant opened the door to let out a man, when he (witness) went in he found Elliott and Charleston; John Haslam, collier, Westhoughton, and Alice Daley, a woman of disrepute, in a different rooms together. Police constable Vance gave evidence of seeing money pass between one of the couples. Charleston told P.S. Rhodes that she was engaged at 'Weston's,' and had lodged at defendant's house for three months – several witnesses were called for the defence. Defendant was fined £10 and costs with the alternative of four months imprisonment with hard labour.

Deansgate, *c.* 1900. (Image courtesy of Chris Driver)

FIVE

A Batch of Disorderly Characters, 1876

(FROM THE *BOLTON WEEKLY JOURNAL*, SATURDAY 12 FEBRUARY 1876)

At the Borough Court, on Monday, several disreputable women were brought up and dealt with as follows – Kate Grace, Moor Lane, for standing in Deansgate with several men and obstructing the footpath, on the 5th inst, was sent to prison for one month; Rebecca Liversey, Moor Lane, for making improper overtures to passengers in Deansgate on the same date, was committed to prison for 14 days; Margaret Cunningham, Black Horse Street, for behaving in a riotous and disorderly manner on Saturday, was sent to prison for one month; and Margaret Howarth, Howell Croft for similar conduct on that date, was committed to prison for two months.

SIX

EXECUTION OF COOPER
– THE BOLTON MURDER, 1879

(FROM THE *BOLTON EVENING NEWS*, 20 MAY 1879)

THIS MORNING

In Strangeways Gaol, this morning, William Cooper, the murderer of Ellen Mather, underwent the last dread penalty of the law for his crime, the memorable words of his victim, 'I hope he'll suffer for it,' being thus painfully realised in his awful and ignominious death. For more than a week it has been known that the execution would take place in private, the representatives of the press, who have hitherto been present at the carrying out of the death sentence being denied 'permits' to the gaol. The High Sheriff of the County, William Garnett, Esq., of Quermore Park, near Lancaster, persistently refused all applications, both personal and by letter, from the newspapers, invariably replying that owing to the altered prison regulations he considered that it was not proper to grant the privileges hitherto accorded to the Press. An appeal from this decision was made to the Home Secretary, but he intimated that he could not interfere, and the consequence was that the execution took place in almost entire privacy. The morbid feeling which invariably attracts to the locality of the prison the crowd of persons who assemble to witness the hoisting of the black flag, the insignia of the dreadful tragedy enacted within its walls, was not wanting in this instance. The neighbourhood of the Assize Court, as early as seven o'clock was the gathering place for a large number of persons. Even at that time there had assembled about a hundred people, who took up their stations on the raising ground opposite the chief entrance to the gaol and in half-an-hour's time that number had increased to between four and five hundred. It was a motley gathering, and, might be taken as not an unfair sample of the dense crowds that assembled to witness the executions of condemned prisoners at the time when they were led out to death face to face with the great crowd of witnesses. Men, women and even young lads that congregated; women with children at the breast sat on a hillock, peering towards the prison, glancing ever and anon at the flag staff near the condemned cell, and then at the clock, as the morning hands showed that slowly but surely the dread preparations were being proceeded with inside, and that when the fatal hour of eight was reached the life of one of their fellow creatures was to be sacrificed to the law. The men were almost all of them of the lowest class, many of them with the stamp of infamy written all too plainly on their faces, whilst here and there workmen with bundles containing their dinners tied up in handkerchiefs, waited on their way to their avocation, to witness the hoisting of the flag. A large building in course of erection near the top of the street, had its eager spectators, from the walls of which, we are informed, some slight view of the prison yard could be obtained. And so the crowd waited until after the chiming of the hour. Five minutes elapsed, another minute passed, and then, at precisely seven minutes past eight, a movement at the skylight at the summit of the building, and at the foot of the flag-staff, was observed, a murmur of excitement passed through the hundreds who were watching everything there was to be

'The gruesome Bolton Murder! Read all about it!'

William Marwood, executioner.

observed, and a policeman was seen to emerge on to the roof, and pull at the rope attached to the pole. In a moment the flag, as dreadful in its significance as it was black in hue, was hoisted to the top of the staff, and a breath of wind springing up amid the calmness of the warm Spring morning, the banner floated in the breeze, telling its own fearful story. This seen, the majority of the crowd descended the slope of the bank, and gradually dispersed. A number of them eagerly followed the representatives of the Press, who were with them watching the flag, as they made their way to the prison gates, and asked to see the chaplain, the Rev. Mr. Draper, or other gentleman in attention who could give them any further facts of the execution. The curiosity of the crowd to peep inside the massive iron gates was but little satisfied. Only an inner quadrangle with ponderous gates opposite could be seen, and then the reporters passed through. In a short time Mr. Draper sent a communication to the effect that he had nothing to say, and the reporters need not stay. Applications was next made to the Governor (Captain Leggett), but that gentleman was at breakfast, and declined to give any information, adding that he might be seen at ten o'clock in the gaol. Two surgeons who witnessed the execution were as reticent to the press representatives, and had 'nothing to say.' Were it not for the information then conveyed by one who was present at the execution, but whose identity shall not be further disclosed for obvious reasons, the public would be in entire ignorance of the facts of the execution. We are enabled to state, however, that the execution took place at two minutes past eight o'clock. At that hour the Under Sheriff, J. Sharp Esq., Lancaster, the Governor of the Gaol, and two or three wardens were near the scaffold waiting for the condemned man, who then arrived with the executioner, Marwood, and attended by the chaplain of the prison, who recited the prayers for the dead, from the burial service. When under the beam he prayed earnestly, 'God have mercy on my soul; God in heaven take care of my family.' Cooper was very firm, and walked with a composed step, exhibiting not a shade of perturbation during the dread ordeal, and not needing the assistance of Marwood who took hold of his arm. Arrived on the drop, Marwood adjusted the rope round the criminal's neck, hastily slipped the white cap over his head, and then, with a nimble backward step, he drew the bolt from its socket, and the drop fell. Instantaneous was the death of the murderer, not a struggle betraying the fact that death had not immediately ensued. The rope swung round the fatal beam, and then all was over. The body hung for an hour, after which it was cut down and the inquest was held before Mr. Price, the county coroner.

Marwood, the executioner, arrived at the gaol on his fatal errand last night about nine o'clock, and at once made his usual preparations. It is said that the condemned man heard the drop tried, and stated that it went like a knife to his heart, but that he soon became hardened and resigned himself to his fate.

This morning, at eight o'clock, the Rev. J.F. Wright, vicar of Christ Church, visited the house of Mr. John Cooper, Commission Street, and prayed with the widow and family of the condemned man; and the Rev. J.G. Doman, M.A., vicar of St. Mark's engaged in prayer with the father and mother of Cooper.

LATER PARTICULARS

As the spectators departed others filled up their places, and there was a goodly number present when the black flag was taken down at nine o'clock precisely. Some persons, possessed of more perseverance than others, lingered still in the hope of catching a glimpse of Marwood as he left the gaol, and ultimately saw him at 11 o'clock depart with two or three persons said to be his relatives living in this neighbourhood. At ten o'clock the Governor of the gaol was waited upon by the reporters to furnish official particulars at the execution, but he firmly declined, stating that 'he was forbidden to communicate anything.' The chaplain however, on being, 'interviewed' later on did not prove quite so reticent; but little could be gleaned from him. He stated that the condemned man passed rather a restless night, and this morning joined earnestly with him in prayer. The prisoner prayed himself fervently for his wife and children, and expressed the utmost contrition for his sins. The sacrament of the Holy Communion was not administered to him, as he did not ask for it.

The *Manchester Evening Mail* has the following:-
Cooper rose before four o'clock this morning, having slept little during the night. He changed his clothes, attiring himself to his own suit in place of the prison garb, which as is usual on such occasions, he was allowed to discard before being led to the scaffold. He than sat down to write, and penned two letters, one of which he addressed to his wife and family, and the other to his brother John. He implored his wife and family always to conduct themselves so that they might be prepared for death, as there was no knowing what a day might bring forth, and said he only hoped that they felt as he did. He told his wife that if she had any 'memory' cards printed he would like them to be in the following form:-

In memory of William Cooper, who departed this life, 20th May, 1879, aged 42 years. Lord, be merciful unto me a sinner.

When gathering clouds around I view,
When days are dark, and friends are few,
On Him I lean, who, not in vain,
Experienced every human pain:
He sees my wants, always my fears,
And counts and treasures up my tears.

And, oh, when I have safely passed,
Through every conflict but the last,
Till, still unchanging, watch beside,
My painful bed – for Thou hast died,
Then point to realms of cloudless day,
And wipe the latest tear away.

In his letter to his brother, the culprit begged him to be kind to his wife and children when he had gone, and urged him for his sake to teach them to do right. The condemned man handed both the letters to the Rev. J. Draper, the chaplain, when he arrived at the gaol at half-past six, and desired him to see that they were delivered into the proper hands. Mr. Draper stayed with him half an hour, and visited him again about half-past seven remaining by his side from that time to the end. Cooper received the ministrations of the rev. gentleman in a becoming manner, but exhibited a strange indifference to his awful fate. The better feelings of his nature seemed to have been stifled, and not the slightest indication of terror was there in his manner.

THE INQUEST

At twelve o'clock the jury had assembled at the prison, and the inquest was held before F. Price, Esq., the county coroner. The jury first visited the mortuary house adjoining the prison hospital, where the body was removed after it was cut down. The body had been placed in a plain deal coffin, and the clothes worn by deceased – the same as he appeared before the magistrates and in which he was hung –

were also placed along with the body. The features of the corpse were discoloured and plainly betokened the manner in which he had met his death. On returning to the jury room the following evidence was taken:-

Silas Denbrow said: I am chief warder at her Majesty's prison at Cheetham. The dead body now shown to their inquest jury is that of William Cooper as the identical body of the man of that name who was late a prisoner under sentence of death. On the 19th March last he was committed by warrant, which I produce, the coroner of the borough of Bolton, and on the 20th of March last by the warrant (which I also produce) of a justice of the peace of the borough of Bolton to this prison to take his trial at the then ensuing assizes for the wilful murder of one Ellen Mather. He was accordingly at the now last assizes held at Manchester for this county, indicted, tried, and convicted of the said offence, and for that offence was sentenced to be hanged by the neck until he was dead. I produce the manuscript delivery of the gaol of this county, held at the Assize Court in Manchester, on Thursday, on the 24th April last, signed by the Clerk of the Assize, in which is recorded the sentence of death passed upon the deceased. I was present this morning, at eight o'clock when judgement of death was duly executed and carried into effect upon the said deceased for the said offence within the walls of this prison, by hanging. The body of deceased remained hanging one hour and was then taken down; and he was then dead and was examined by the surgeon of this prison. There was no deviation in this case from the usual method of hanging persons sentence to death, which was carried into effect by the executioner appointed by the Sheriff. The deceased man was a brass moulder, and was 42 years of age.

Charles Hitchman Braddon said: I am the surgeon of this prison. I was present at eight o'clock this morning when sentence of death was carried into effect upon the prisoner, William Cooper, by hanging. I examined the body of the deceased immediately after the execution, and I found it to be dead. Death was caused by fracture of the neck, and took place instantaneously.

This was all the evidence, and the jury immediately returned as their verdict that the cause of death was 'Fracture of the neck by hanging, in pursuance of the sentence of the law.'

We are indebted for the above evidence to the Coroner, as reporters were not admitted, a fact which was the cause of some surprise to the jurymen, who asked why they were not present, and were told that they were not allowed to be present on this occasion.

COOPER'S CRIME

The crime for which Cooper suffered the extreme penalty of the law was committed nine weeks ago, viz., on the night of St. Patrick's Day, Monday March 17th. As its recital in all its dread details has since that time thrilled with horror the inhabitants of the town, and the narrative is fresh in the recollection of all, it will unnecessary as well as unwise to do more than briefly recount the incidents. William Cooper, a man of 42, of Forge Street, foreman brass moulder, formed an attachment more than twenty years ago with a barmaid named Ellen Smith, employed at Mrs. Leach's Albert Inn, Derby Street, an attachment which, governed and unrestrained, under circumstances which ought to have crushed it out of being, culminated in this shocking tragedy. Little more than a boy and a girl at the time, the inevitable lovers quarrel took place, and Cooper, in a fit of pique or pride, or both, as scores of young and ardent swains have done before, enlisted for a soldier in a regiment under the service of the East India Company. Two years of absence from his native land ensued, and then his release from military life, owing to the English Government superseding the East India Company, enabled him to return to England, where he was doomed to undergo the mortification of finding that this former sweetheart had married a moulder named James Mather; and, as if to increase the aggravation, only the day before his arrival. Shortly after this, Cooper himself married but the attachment to his former sweetheart seems to have returned, if indeed it ever left him, and the acquaintance, though nothing absolutely criminal is alleged, was renewed. In 1872 Mrs. Mather's husband went to America, taking with him his three sons and leaving with his wife the youngest child, now aged nine. She then returned as a barmaid to the Albert Inn, handing the child over to the care of her mother. Since that time Cooper continued his attentions, and up to the shocking event which terminated their relationship, was almost a nightly visitor at the house where she served. On the evening of St. Patrick's Day Mrs. Leach acted as caterer at the ball held at the Baths Assembly Rooms, and had desired Mrs. Wareing, her sister, and Mrs. Mather to go the Baths after closing time at the inn, to assist in the waiting. Cooper, who had been, as usual, at the house, learned that Mrs. Mather was about to go to the Baths, and, for some reason which has never been satisfactorily explained, he appeared determined that she should not attend, and waited for the pair at the bottom of Derby Street. He there asked them where they were going, and they told him. He persisted that Mrs. Mather should not go, but after a wordy altercation to proceed, he struck her. By this time the trio had walked past Trinity Church in the direction of the Baths in Bridgeman Street. On arriving on the pavement opposite the entrance to the station steps on the Church side of the street, Cooper seized Mrs. Mather, and after a brief struggle severed her jugular vein with a pocket knife, the women falling to the floor in a bleeding and fainting condition. Mrs. Wareing screamed for assistance, and Cooper then gave himself up to the first police officer who arrived, to whom he affirmed that he had killed the woman, and that he always intended to do it, adding on his way for years, 'morn, noon, and night.' His victim was conveyed to the surgery of Dr. Johnson, where her deposition was taken in the presence of the prisoner who had to be removed from the cells for the purpose. The poor woman, who in her deposition said Cooper was a bad one and she hoped he would suffer for what he had done, expired the following morning at the Infirmary about half-past eleven, having lingered nearly twelve hours. The inquest was held on the Wednesday before Mr. R. Taylor, the borough coroner, at which the only verdict that could be arrived at upon the evidence; that of 'Wilful Murder,' was returned, and on the day following the prisoner Alderman C. Wolfenden, W. Hesketh, and Joseph Musgrave, R. Stockdale, C Heaton, and W. Smith Esq., Dr. Livy and Captain Fell, committed for trial upon the capital charge. On Monday, April 28, the trial at the Manchester Assizes took place before Mr. Justice Stephen. Mr. Lereache, barrister, instructed by Mr. John Hall, public prosecutor, prosecuted, and Mr. Addison, instructed by Mr, M. Fielding, solicitor, defended. The facts of the case were fully investigated, all that could be said for the accused was advanced by his counsel, and the Judge gave an exhaustive and masterly definition of

A constable surveys the scene of the crime.

what constituted the crime of murder in the eye of the law. The case was then left with the jury, who, after a few minutes consultation, found him guilty. His Lordship, in passing sentence of death, amid the breathless stillness of a crowded court, said the prisoner had been convicted upon evidence so clear and so full that the jury would have been wanting to their sworn duty if they had returned any other verdict whatever. It must be obvious to all that he nourished for the woman an unlawful passion, that he allowed that unlawful passion to pass as it so often did, into a form of cruelty, and that at last the woman whom he thought he loved died by his hand.

Since his committal Cooper has paid great attention to the ministration of the chaplain of Strangeways Gaol, the Rev. John Draper. He has been visited several times by the Rev. J.G. Doman, M.A., vicar of St. Mark's, Bolton, in whose parish the deceased with his family lived, and who has taken great interest in the family, and the Rev. J.F. Wright, of Christ Church, Bolton. On Saturday, May 3rd, Cooper's father and mother visited him, and on the following Tuesday his wife and four children paid him a visit, the latter, which took place in the presence of wardens, lasting over an hour and three quarters, a most affecting incident occurring at the close. The youngest child, which had been its father's pet, desired to stay with him, and share his hard bed and the prison diet, but this could not be allowed, and the child had to submit to be removed. On Friday, the 9th instant, an interview took place between Cooper and his brother and sister-in-law, and on Saturday, the 10th, Mr. Richard Beckett, of the Founders Arms, Ashburner Street, Bolton, saw him, he being cordially received by the culprit, who discoursed with him at length respecting his wife and family. Later on in the same day Robert Jones, Thomas Carter and Richard Banks, of Bolton, George Taylor, Wigan, and Joseph Morris, Bury, formerly fellow workmen or old acquaintances of Cooper's visited him, and to them he expressed his deep sorrow for the crime and hopes of divine forgiveness. He also saw his sister Mrs. Bates, of Reddish, and her husband, and on Wednesday he had an interview with his eldest brother, Mr. John Cooper, of Commission Street. On Saturday the final interview took place, the prisoner seeing on that occasion for the last time, his wife and six children, his brother (John Cooper), and Mrs. Cooper's sister (Mrs. Wood, of Bolton). This interview lasted two hours and a half, and was a most painful one.

SEVEN

SHOCKING DISCOVERY IN LEICESTER STREET, 1879

(FROM THE *BOLTON JOURNAL*, SATURDAY 6 SEPTEMBER 1879)

R Taylor Esq., Borough Coroner, held an inquest at the Town Hall, on Tuesday, on the body of Carolin Moscrop, three years of age, daughter of James Moscrop, labourer, Tower Street, who was found dead on Sunday morning. Hannah Moscrop, mother of the deceased, said she saw the child alive and well on Saturday morning at eleven o'clock, but missed it shortly afterwards, and went several times to the Police Office. On Sunday evening a milkman told her the child had been found in a closet. Heather Emery, 68 Leicester Street, said that on Sunday morning her husband was looking for a large pan. They both went into an empty house, and her husband found the missing child in the closet. Deceased was lying on the side of the face with its legs up. The lid was down. A Mr. Crankshaw arrived and got the child out. Life was extinct. John H. Crankshaw, Arkwright Street, said that at a quarter to nine on Sunday Morning he was sent for to Leicester Street, where he found a child in the closet bucket, with its face towards the front. The bucket contained about a half a gill of water. The deceased's back was bent backwards as if she had fallen in. There was an appearance of a struggle for breath. There were no marks of violence upon the body. He believed death was purely through accident. He recollected seeing a marble in the bucket, and he believed an attempt had been made by the child to recover something. A juryman asked if there was any medical testimony, as he had heard the child had been abused. Witness said there were no marks of violence whatever upon the body, except discolouration through the position of the child, and found no marks of violence upon the body. One of the jury said there was such a small quantity of water in the pan, he could not understand how it would have been suffocated. The coroner thought it would have been smothered if there had been no water in whatever. Another juryman thought a post mortem examination of the body should be made, as there had been a rumour of something unfair having taken place, the inquest was adjoined in order to allow a post mortem examination to be made by the Medical Officer of Health. On Wednesday Mr. Edw. Sergeant said that on Tuesday afternoon he made a post mortem examination of the body and found a bruise on the left thigh, with excoriations upon the left side of the face and nose. In the mouth were small particles of grit and cinder. The lungs were very much congested; the other organs were perfectly healthy. In his opinion death took place from suffocation. There were no marks whatever of any violation of the child. Deceased had fallen into an awkward position in the bucket, and was unable to breathe. The jury returned a verdict of 'Accidental Suffocation.'

EIGHT

ALLEGED FATAL FIGHT AT CHEW MOOR, 1879

(FROM THE *JOURNAL*, SATURDAY 5 JULY 1879)

A sad event has taken place at Chew Moor, Lostock, a man named Edmund Whowell, collier of Spinner's Row, having died through injuries he received whilst fighting with George Holden, gardener, the Hillock. From inquiries we have made it appears that on Saturday night between nine and ten o'clock, Holden was in the Black Horse Street beer house, and there were two other men in company with him, when Whowell came into the room. Holden hospitably offered his glass of beer to him, so that he could drink, but Whowell, who was the worse for liquor, instead of reciprocating this friendly overture, dashed the contents of the glass into the fireplace, and threatened to hurl the glass at Holden's head. A few words followed, and then Holden left the beer house to go home. Whowell immediately went after him, challenged him to fight, and followed him towards his home. When near the bridge that crosses the railway, in the opposite direction to Whowell's residence, the men commenced to fight. Whowell was the younger man, being about 35, whilst his antagonist is 45 years of age, but he being the most intoxicated he soon succumbed, and whilst on the ground Holden kicked him about the head. Two spinners from Lostock, who were returning from a walk, saw the men at this point, but being strangers did not like to interfere beyond calling upon the men to desist. A neighbour named George Fletcher, who came up at this time, had, however, no such scruples, and separated the men, who went to their respective homes. Whowell was able to go out on Sunday morning, and told one of his friends that he should not be able to recognise the man with whom he had been fighting. In the afternoon the pain in his head became worse, and he went to bed, and passed such a painful night that Bringloe, of Westhoughton, was summoned on Monday morning. The gentleman did not anticipate then that the injuries would be fatal, but when he paid a second visit to deceased shortly before nine o'clock on Tuesday morning, he was rapidly sinking, and died in a few minutes after his arrival. Mr. Bringloe then informed Bolton constable Bardsley, who is stationed at Chew Moor, of what had taken place; and that officer apprehended Holden as he was proceeding to the residence of Whowell to inquire as to his condition. There seems to have been no enmity between the two, and both men bear the character of quiet, steady men. It is a matter of remark now that Holden has been teetotal for twelve months, but broke his pledge at Wigan fair. The deceased was employed at the Brigadier Pit of the Syndale Hall Colliery Co., and has only been living at Chew Moor since April, having come there from Darwin. Deceased leaves a wife and four children, the eldest of whom is 14 years of age. Holden is also married, and has several children, his wife, who has been in weak health for some time, was utterly prostrated with the news of her husband's position. The occurrence has caused much interest in the village, where Holden is well known.

THE ACCUSED BEFORE THE MAGISTRATES

Holden was charged before the County Justice, at the Sessions on Thursday morning, with having caused the death of Whowell. Mr. Fielding appeared for the prisoner.

Mr. Superintendent Holland said the prisoner was in custody charged with having caused the death of a person named Edward Whowell, of Lostock. It appeared that there two men were in a beer house on Saturday evening, somewhere between nine and ten o'clock, when some dispute took place between them. They went out, and when a short distance from the beer house they began to fight. The prisoner knocked the deceased down, he was informed, and kicked him, causing considerable injuries. Dr. Bringloe was called in two in three days after, and the deceased died from those injuries on Tuesday morning. The matter had been reported to the Coroner, and he had fixed to hold the inquest at half-past

CIVIC CENTRE, BOLTON

The Magistrate's Court at Bolton.

one in the afternoon, a post mortem examination to be made in the meantime. His application was for a remand. He had a witness in Court who saw part of the fight.

Mr. Fielding said his application was that the Bench admit this prisoner to bail. It appeared that on Saturday night that the prisoner was in the Black Horse beerhouse, Chew Moor, having a glass of beer. He had been there about half an hour when the deceased came in. Deceased was not known to the prisoner, and so far as prisoner knew he was not known to the deceased. He came and sat near the prisoner and asked for some beer. The prisoner generously offered him his glass and said 'drink of this.' At that time deceased had been talking of fighting, and prisoner said 'we want no fighting here, take my glass and drink, and let's be friends.' The deceased then threw the contents in the fireplace, and said 'I have a good mind to throw the glass at your head.' Prisoner said, 'If this is to go on I will go home.' He made towards his home, and the deceased, who lived in the opposite direction, followed him, threatened him, and wanted to fight. He then struck prisoner, who at last said, 'If you insist upon it, and won't let me go away without fighting, I suppose I must fight.' The prisoner was knocked down and seriously injured, and deceased was afterwards knocked down, and he said the injuries were caused by falling upon a stone, and that the prisoner was not responsible for it. If it was manslaughter it was of the mildest kind, and their worships would be justified in granting bail.

George Fletcher was then called, and said he lived at Chew Moor, Lostock, and was a collier. He was in the Black Horse when Whowell came in on Saturday night. Whowell came and sat down next to Holden, and Holden asked him to drink out his glass, and he got hold of it and threw the contents upon the fire. He then said, 'I have a good mind to break your head with the glass for offering it to me to drink out of.' He (witness) had not been in above three or four minutes when Whowell came in. Holden sat still about two or three minutes and then tapped Whowell on the face with the back of his hand. Mrs. Ainscow said she would have no fighting there and they must go out, and they went out. They both said no one must come near them, they would have it out themselves. They went about 60 yards from the beer house, and there commenced fighting. Holden shoved Whowell first, and he fell against the wall, after which they commenced fighting on the floor. He ran to them, and said 'Holden, do no more to him, you have done enough.' He replied, 'Mun I gi' o'er', and witness told him to do so, and took him a few yards off. He then returned, raised Whowell, and took him home. The doctor was called in on Monday morning.

Prisoner was then remanded until Monday, bail being allowed, himself in £50 and two sureties in £25 each.

THE INQUEST

The district coroner, Mr. J. H. Edge, held an inquest on Thursday, at the Wellington Inn, Chew Moor, to enquire into the circumstances attending the death of Whowell. Mr. Fielding, solicitor, watched the proceedings on behalf of Holden.

Mary Whowell, wife of deceased, said: My husband's age is 37. He is a collier. He was brought home on Saturday night a little after 10 o'clock, in a very drunken state, by George Fletcher and another man whom I don't know. He was bleeding from a wound on his eyebrow. He spoke sensibly to me and asked, 'Who has done this?' I replied, 'I don't know, only what these men have told me.' I washed his face, and noticed a cut over his right eye. I could see that his forehead was scarred, and he complained very much of it. It bled a little there. I did not notice any other marks, except scars on his face, and his eyes were black, being much swollen, and he could scarcely open them. Both eyes were black. I got him to bed as soon as I could, and he fell asleep, awaking again at two o'clock on Sunday morning. He complained then of being sore, and of having pain in his head and his shoulder. He got out of bed, and asked me to bathe his face and forehead with cold water, which I did. He afterwards went to bed but could not sleep. He got up on Sunday morning about seven o'clock, washed himself, and bathed his forehead with water. He again asked who had done it. He went out during the morning, and at noon he went out to have a pint of beer, and he also had a gill of porter, thinking it would revive him. He had a little dinner. He went to bed in the afternoon, and got up at half-past six o'clock, when he had a little tea. He went to bed again at eight o'clock, but was restless all night, and complained of being faint, and having great pain in his head. I sent for Dr. Bringloe about five o'clock in the morning, and the doctor saw my husband about eight o'clock. My husband was sensible then and remained so up to eight on Monday night. He never appeared to awake after that time and died about nine o'clock on Tuesday morning. Examined by Mr. Fielding: We have lived here for three months, and came from near Darwin. My husband was not a prize wrestler. He wrestled once for a wager. I have forgotten what the wager was. I cannot say whether it was for £25 a side. He was not drunk on the Sunday.

George Fletcher, collier, Chew Moor, said: I have known deceased for about three months. Last Saturday night I saw him in the Black Horse beer house, Chew Moor. Peter Holden was in the beer house. Deceased came into the kitchen of the beer house at twenty minutes to ten o'clock, and Holden was sitting there. Deceased was very drunk. Holden did not appear to have had much. Deceased sat down next to Holden, and the latter said: 'Will theaw drink wi' me eawt of this glass?' at the same time handing him the glass, which was half full of beer. Instead of drinking the beer deceased threw it into the fire, and said to Holden, 'I have a good mind to break th' head with this glass.' Holden asked deceased if he were going to pay for the beer he had thrown away, but deceased refused. Holden sat quiet two or three minutes, and then tapped deceased on the face with the back of his hand. The landlady, Mrs. Ainscow, then came into the room and ordered them out remarking that there must be no bother there. Holden got up to go out, and deceased followed him, saying, 'We will go and have it out now.' Both men said, when they were going out 'No one came near us.' I and Wm. Swindley followed them. Holden pushed deceased against the wall of the railway bridge. Deceased's face went against the wall. They commenced then to struggle in the lane, and deceased went to the ground. Whilst deceased was down Holden commenced 'punching' him. He kicked him three times, once on the breast and twice on the shoulder. I got hold of Holden's arm and pulled him away, and said, 'Peter, you've done enough at him, let him alone.' Holden then said, 'I will give over and go away,' and I took him away four or five yards. I then went back to deceased, and found he was bleeding from the forehead. He was laid on his side, and was helpless. I sent for his wife, and I took him home. I was between 40 and 50 yards from him when he fell. I could see them staggering together, but could not say how deceased fell, whether it was on his face or not. The road is cindered, with stone intermixed, which were laid bare with rain. Examined by Mr. Fielding: I have known Holden for seven years. Deceased was very drunk when he came into the beer house. Deceased did not say that he wanted to fight before he dashed the beer away. I heard Holden tell deceased not to bother about fighting, but that was after the beer had been thrown away. Deceased replied 'I've a good mind to split your head with the glass.' Up to that time Holden had not given a word of offence, except asking deceased to pay for the beer. Holden tapped deceased on the face; it was not a stroke of the hand on the face. Holden did not say 'I will be going home.' The landlady came in when deceased threatened Holden. I and Swindley stayed behind. Both men fell, and Holden was at the top. It was not a very dark night. I did not see deceased push Holden. I do not know whether there were any 'clinkers' on the road. Deceased was not sensible when I took him home. I saw deceased on the Sunday morning at nine o'clock. He said, 'George, where is that man I was agate with last night?' I said, 'Ned, what deal want!' He rejoined, 'I intend to have it out with him.' I said 'Take my advice and don't go near, for it is a disgrace to fight on Sunday morning.' Deceased then remarked, 'I will go home and take your advice.' I was four or five yards away when the kicks were given. I did not see him kicked on the forehead. The wound might have been caused by falling.

Capel William Bringloe said, 'I am a licentiate of the faculty of physicians and surgeons, Glasgow, in practice in Westhoughton. I was called to see this man on Monday morning, the message reaching me about five o'clock. He was in bed, and complained of intense pain in his head, and of being sore all over his body. I noticed that he had an abrasion on the centre of the forehead, a slight cut over the right eyebrow, abrasion under the right eye, and an abrasion below the left eye. His face was rauch swollen and his eyes were very black. I prescribed for him and saw him again about nine o'clock on Tuesday morning. He was then in a comatose condition, and was dying. I made a post mortem examination this morning with the assistance of Dr. Settle. I found that there were several marks of external injury over the head. In addition to the injuries already mentioned, there was a large swelling under the ear on the right side of the neck. The lower portion of the body was swollen and bruised. The left shoulder and chest were very much bruised. On removing the scalp I found very extensive congestion, but no effusion on the skull. The covering of the brain was highly congested, but there was no effusion on the surface of the brain. All the ventricles of the brain were full of bloody serum. In the third ventricle there was a large clot of blood. There was no appearance of disease. On examination of the chest I found a very slight effusion of serum in the bag of the heart. All the lungs, and the other organs were empty. The body was decomposing very rapidly. Deceased was a strong man, and the body was well nourished. In my opinion the cause of death was effusion of blood in the third ventricle of the brain. This would probably by caused by outward violence. A blow or a fall might cause it. The wound below the right ear might have caused this effusion, but I cannot say that any particular wound did cause it. The bruise on the neck might have been caused by a fall on a rough surface. A violent push against the wall might possibly cause the bruise. If the face had been rubbed on the cinder road that would account for the scars. Examined by Mr. Fielding: Two men falling together on small stones might cause the injuries on the face; also that on the neck if there was excessive violence, but it was not as likely. By a Juryman: If a man fell by himself on the edging stones I do not think the fall would have occasioned the injury to the neck.

George Batten, engine tender, Lostock, stated: I saw deceased and Holden come out of the Black Horse beer house, about a quarter to 10 o'clock. I did not know either of them. They appeared to go up to the lane friendly. One man said at the door, 'Come along,' but I don't who made the remark. Both men appeared to have had drink. When they got between the railway walls they made a stand. They both got hold, and one pushed the other against the wall, and then both fell to the ground. I went towards them, and the tallest man got to his feet and kicked the man on the ground, still keeping hold of his shoulder. He kicked him several times, but I can't say how many. He kicked him on the head. The man on the floor struggled, and he that was standing up kicked him on the shoulder and in the side. The man on the ground got up, and they seized one another again, and both fell to the ground. They rose, and fell again, but the taller man managed to get to his feet, and kicked the other man in the side. I said, 'Is there anyone here who can part these men; I will fetch the police.' Fletcher then took the taller man away. I then went home. I had not been in the beer house, and did not know either of the men. Examined by Mr. Fielding: I had been in no other beer house. The affair only occupied two or three minutes. I was with William Morris. We were strangers, and did not like to interfere. I saw them fall three times. The first kicking I believe, was on the side of the head.

William Morris, spinner, Lostock Junction, supported the evidence of that last witness and said: I knew Holden by name and the other man by sight. Deceased was the first to get hold. I did not see where Holden kicked deceased when Holden got up the first time. I begged Holden to give o'er and got Fletcher to take him away. Examined by Mr. Fielding: I am sure that deceased got hold of Holden first. Holden was walking on quietly. Batten was in front of me. Deceased overtook Holden, who was five or six yards ahead of him. The fight did not last above three minutes.

Edward Blackloe, under-gardener for Mr. Lythgoe, Lostock Junction, said: I was in the Black Horse beer house on Saturday night when deceased came in. He was drunk, and said to Holden, 'Let me drink.' Holden gave the glass to deceased, who threw the contents into the fire. Deceased refused to pay for the beer, and threatened to break Holden's skull. They bothered together a little, and Holden tapped deceased on the face. Mrs. Ainscow came in at the time, and said that she would have no fighting there. Both then went out. I saw them fighting, but could not distinguish them one from another. Examined by Mr. Fielding; I did not hear the conversation about the fighting. All was quiet in the house until deceased came in.

The Coroner, in addressing the jury, said that there were only two questions to be considered by them, and they seemed to him to be very simple. The first was, were they satisfied that the death of deceased was caused by some violence he received on Saturday night. It did not matter what the particular wound that caused death, for as these parties were engaged in an illegal proceeding, Holden was responsible for the death if it resulted from anything that took place then, for the law did not allow men to go out and fight in anger. If it had been a friendly wrestle, and death occurred, it would have been death by misadventure, but if men want to fight a quarrel out, or to fight for a wager, and in the course of that fight, whether by a blow or fall, it was perfectly immaterial, injuries were caused that led to death, the surviving was guilty of manslaughter. The other question to be considered: Did these men go out to decide a dispute between them? The evidence, he thought, was so strong on that point that he did not need to address them upon it. It not appear that Holden had any ill-blood against deceased, but that did not enter into their province to discuss. Were they satisfied that deceased died from injuries received somehow on the night in question, and if so, were they inflicted by Holden? If they were so satisfied their verdict must be one of manslaughter. They must remember that Holden was not to be tried by them. They were merely to inquire the cause of death, and whether explanation there might be for Holden's conduct would have to be addressed to another court. He thought that they would only be doing their duty by finding a verdict of manslaughter, and then leave it to the judge, if Holden was found guilty, to apportion the sentence according to the provocation he (the judge) might think Holden had received.

After deliberating about ten minutes, the jury returned their opinion that deceased had been 'unlawfully and feloniously killed and slain by Peter Holden.'

The Coroner then told Holden that it was his duty to commit him to take his trial at the next Manchester Assizes on a charge of manslaughter.

On the application of Mr. Fielding, the Coroner accepted the same bail for Holden as was received by the magistrates.

SUMMARY OF THE TRIAL – THE FATAL FIGHT AT CHEW MOOR

At the County Sessions on Monday afternoon, Peter Holden, gardener of Chew Moor, was charged on remand with having caused the death of Edmund Whowell, collier, aged 37, of Spinners Row, Chew Moor. The occurrence which has resulted so fatally took place on Saturday, the 28th. About ten o'clock on the night of that day the parties left the Black Horse beer house, Chew Moor, and after proceeding a few yards commenced to fight. The fight lasted only a few minutes, but the men were up and down three times, and whilst Whowell was on the ground it is alleged that Holden kicked him on the head and shoulder. Whowell was able to go about on Sunday, but on Monday, Dr. Bringloe, junr., of Westhoughton was summoned, but Whowell succumbed to his injuries on Tuesday morning. An inquest was held on Thursday, when it was shown that Whowell commenced the quarrel by throwing Holden's beer into the fireplace, and that there had been no previous ill-feeling between them. The jury returned a verdict of manslaughter, and Holden was committed to the Assizes on the coroner warrant. Mr. Fielding watched the examination on behalf of Holden. The same evidence as was given at the inquest was rejected. The only additional witness called was P.C. Bardsley, who said he apprehended prisoner on Tuesday morning, at a quarter past nine o'clock, and brought him to the County Police Station, Bolton. He charged him with the offence, and prisoner made no reply. Prisoner had nothing to say, and Mr. Fielding observed that he supposed no observations of his would alter the determination of the Bench to send Holden for trial. Mr. Briggs, presiding magistrate, said they had no discretion but to send him for trial. Mr. Fielding said they might come to the conclusion that the death was by misadventure, and not by an act of violence of the prisoner. He submitted that the case stood thus: Prisoner left the beer house and was followed by deceased, who got hold of prisoner, and they fell. Up to that time prisoner had taken no active measures. They fell on stones, prisoner being at the top, and he (Mr. Fielding) should say that the injury to the head was caused in that fashion. They had it in evidence that on the Sunday deceased had drink which caused excitement, and might be the cause of the rush of blood to the brain. If they took his view the death was by misadventure. Mr. Briggs said that taking all the circumstances of the case into consideration they were bound to send the case for trial by a jury, and prisoner would, therefore, be committed to the Assizes. Prisoner was admitted to bail.

(FROM THE *JOURNAL*, SATURDAY 5 JULY 1879)

MANCHESTER SUMMER ASSIZES
CROWN COURT – SATURDAY.
BEFORE MR. JUSTICE BOWEN
THE FATAL FIGHT AT LOSTOCK

Peter Holden, indicted for having at Lostock, on the 1st instant, feloniously killed and slain Edward Whowell, was placed in the dock and pleaded guilty to the indictment. Mr. Nash prosecuted, and Mr. Addison defended. Mr. Addison, in mitigation of the sentence, urged that the prisoner was most inoffensive and a person of good character, which would be spoke to by his employer Mr Adam Riddick, of Bolton. On the day in question the prisoner called at a public house in Lostock, where he saw the deceased in a drunken state, and who, without any provocation, threw a glass of beer upon the prisoner and at the same time said he had a good mind to break his head. Thereupon prisoner remonstrated with the

The Dock.

deceased, and subsequently the parties fought together in the street. They fought for some time in the Lancashire style, which was known as 'up and down,' and a style similar to that adopted in France. In this instance he could not acknowledge that they managed those things better in France. In the course of the struggle deceased received a blow on the head, which caused an effusion of blood upon the brain, and as he went on drinking for two days, he died on the Tuesday night after the fight took place. Under all the circumstances, Mr. Addison thought this was not a case in which there was any criminal intention.

His Lordship deferred sentenced.

THE LOSTOCK MANSLAUGHTER

Peter Holden, 45, for manslaughter at Lostock, on the 1st July, was sentenced to six calendar months hard labour.

NINE

ALLEGED MURDER IN BOLTON, 1880

(FROM THE *JOURNAL*, SATURDAY 31 JULY 1880)

THE INQUEST

Rowland Taylor, Esq., borough coroner, held an inquest on Monday morning at the Town Hall, to inquire into the circumstances of the death of John Stewart, labourer, of 126, Canon Street, who died on Thursday from injuries he received on Friday, the 26th June last. The following evidence was given:

Robert Stewart, painter, 126, Canon Street, said: Deceased was my brother. He was 50 last birthday. He was a coalheaver, and went out with coal carts. I had not seen him for some time before the 26th June. On that day he came to my house, having a wound on his head, of which he complained. He asked me for 2d., to pay for his lodgings, and I replied that he wanted it for drink. He repeated that he owed his landlady 2d., and he wanted to pay to be quit of her, for she had given him his death-blow this time. A lodger in my house said: 'Here, John, I will give 2d.' I did not see my brother again until the 2nd of July. He was at Joseph Clemmett's beer house lying on the sofa speechless, and I took him to my house, where he died last Thursday. Mr. Dorrian attended him when he was at my house. My brother has taken drink and made straight with all he got. He told me that his landlady hit him with a poker. He was quite sensible at the time.

Joseph Clemmett, 131, Deansgate, Queen's Arms beer house, said: 'On the 25th June, at 11.15 pm deceased came to my house. We were gone upstairs, but I came down owing to the continuous knocking, and found deceased outside with his face covered with blood.' He said: 'Yon old Irishwoman has hit me on the top of the head with poker.' I said: 'Which Irishwoman?' and he replied 'Mrs Maddon.' He asked me to go down with him to the lodging house, and I refused, telling him that they might hit me. I advised deceased to go with me to another lodging house, and found him a place at Mrs. Kilroy's in Queen Street. I paid 6d., for his lodgings. I saw deceased in the street the following morning, and he told me that he was very poorly. On the night of that day I gave him 4d., for his lodgings. On the Sunday deceased came to my house, and complained of being ill, and my wife gave him his dinner. I gave him money also for that night's lodgings, and arranged with him to do some white washing on the Monday, but he was unable to do it. On the Tuesday he white washed the back yard, but complained of his head, and the same on Wednesday. When having his dinner on Wednesday deceased appeared to become paralysed, and I gave him some tea and brandy. He stayed on the sofa until eight o'clock, and then went out. I had given him half-a-crown. On the Thursday he came to my house, but could not work, and laid on the sofa all day. He went to the lodging house again at night, and on the Friday he came again, and appearing to become worse I sent for his relations, who took him away.

Hannah Wilson, 12, Idle Lane, said: 'I remember the 25th June, I heard a row at half-past ten o'clock at night, and I looked through the bedroom window with a candle in my hand. I saw Mrs Maddon strike deceased on the head. I cannot say what she struck him with. I ran downstairs and saw deceased outside on the ground bleeding fearfully from a gash in his head. Mrs. Maddon, who had gone towards her own house, came back again to deceased. I bathed the wound of deceased with warm water. I cannot say whether he was drunk. I did not see his hand near Mrs. Maddon. It was a dark night, but I could see them because I had a candle. There was only one wound upon deceased. Mrs. Maddon said she had struck deceased with a spoon, because he would not pay her 2d. I showed the police officer the wound when he came. I and Mrs. Maddon are good friends. I have known her for some six years.

Mary Ironfield, wife of John Ironfield, Gibbon's Court, off Idle Lane, said: 'On the 25th of June I saw this row. I was in Idle Lane, and I saw Mrs. Maddon pushing deceased out of her house. I knew both of them. I heard her say to deceased that he owed her 2d., and he replied that he had not got it, but should have it tomorrow. She then pushed him out of the house, and up the lane as far as No. 14. He stood against the house, and she struck him once or twice, but I cannot say what with. She then went away, and afterwards came back with a candle in her hand to look at him. She said: 'I have not done him any harm,' although he was 'bleeding like a pig.' Deceased had had drink, but was not drunk. He did not fall until Mrs. Maddon hit him. He did not strike or pull Mrs. Maddon.

Ann Whiteley, widow, 12, Albion Court, Idle Lane, said: 'On the 25th June, I and my daughter were going down Idle Lane, at half-past-ten o'clock. I saw an old man coming up quickly up the lane and Mrs. Maddon after him. She would be half a yard behind him. She had a candle in her hand, and something in the other. I saw her strike him on the head, and he fell. It was a piece of iron of some sort, but not a poker, that she struck him with. I told her that it was a shame to strike anyone with a weapon like that. I only saw her strike him once. Mrs Maddon and I are friends. The iron was something like a 'cow-rake' handle.

P.C. Austin: I was on duty in Deansgate on the night of the 25th June. I was going past Idle Lane when I heard a noise, and going down the lane I noticed a man sitting on the footpath. The man was cursing. He was bleeding from the head, and I asked him what had caused it. He said, 'Mrs. Maddon has struck me with a poker, because I had not money to pay my lodgings.' I left him and went into Mrs. Maddon's and asked her if she had struck him with a poker, She replied, 'No, I struck him with this spoon,' showing me an ordinary metal spoon. 'I struck him,' she said 'because he came into the house and was throttling me.' When I came out of Mrs. Maddon's the man was gone. I thought the man was far gone in drink.

Mr. J. Dorrian, surgeon, Blackburn Street, said: 'I saw deceased on the 6th of this month when he called at my surgery to consult me about an injury which he had received to his head. I examined the wound, which was on the top of the head, inclining to the left side. It was an incised wound, about four inches in length. The hair had been shaved off, and the wound was perfectly healed: and no appearance of inflammation or bruise. I gave him some medicine, and recommended him to go home and keep quiet. I asked him how it occurred. He told me that he lodged with Mrs. Maddon, 20, Idle Lane, whom I knew, and that he and her had had some quarrel a few days before as to a son who had enlisted, and that she had struck him with a coal shovel. The blow had made him feel week and poorly. He called upon me twice afterwards, and I told him and his friend that although the wound had healed I considered his case a serious one, for fear of inflammation in the brain or membranes supervening. He was perfectly sensible, but the mouth was drawn a little on one side. It was that fact that made me consider his case serious. About eight days before the day of his death, he was taken home, complaining of pain in his head. Leeches were applied and perfect rest ordered. During Wednesday evening, the 21st inst., he became worse, and on the following day he was unconscious, and died the same day. By your order a post mortem examination was made by me, with the assistance of Dr. Mallett, on Friday last, and except the wound already named there was no external injury to the body. Under the wound there was no inflammation. It had healed satisfactorily. On exposing the brain, and exactly corresponding with the external wound there was an abscess five inches in length and three inches in width, lying on the surface of the brain, under the covering. On opening that we found it to contain from 2 to 2.5 oz of pus or matter. Under it the brain was indented with the pressure, but otherwise the left and right side, inside and out, were quite healthy. Dr. Mallett and I examined the chest. The lungs were found to be sound, but on the left and right side there were pleuratic adhesions. The heart was healthy and sound, and all the abdominal viscera in their normal condition. The cause of death was the external wound on the scalp. Although the wound was perfectly healed, slow inflammation of the membrane of the brain supervened, terminating in an abscess, which produced coma and death. Abscess is sometimes the result of disease of the brain, but in this case the brain was perfectly healthy. Deceased was altogether a sound man. One blow of this (producing the tablespoon) could not have caused the wound, as it is circular. Two blows might have done it.

James Brown, lodging in King Street, said: On Friday, the 25th June, I was in Mrs. Maddon's when deceased came in. He was very drunk and rough, and cursed her. She said that had trouble enough on her mind through her son, and that he must either sit down or go to bed. She, however, put him out quietly, but he returned in a rougher state than ever. She had a spoon in one hand and a candle in the other. He caught her by the throat and then by her clothes, and pulled her out of the house. They both came in again, and deceased said: 'Mrs. Maddon, you have caught me on the old wound which I got at Squire Hulton's.' He told me about the wound a fortnight previous. I had spoken to him about his drinking.

Mr. Dorrian, re-examined, said: The injury that caused the death was recent; the abscess was recent. Brown: He did not tell me when the wound was received.

Mr. Clemmett: Deceased had not worked in the coalpit for 10 years.

Dr. Dorrian: I have not heard of the old wound before. A wound ten to twelve years ago might have produced the abscess. One of the jurymen has asked me if the handle of a spoon would not have produced the last wound, I say it might have done.

The Coroner said he thought they could give no other verdict than that it was a case of manslaughter. There was direct evidence that a blow had been given, and that the blow had killed him. He could see no reason for bringing in a verdict of death by inadvertence.

A verdict of manslaughter against Maddon was then returned.

PRISONER BEFORE THE MAGISTRATE

Immediately after the inquest Ann Maddon, widow, lodging house keeper, 20 Idle Lane, was charged before the magistrates with the manslaughter of deceased, the magistrates being Alderman Walmsley and Wolfenden and Captain Fell.

Mr. Hall said prisoner was charged with the manslaughter of a lodger of hers, whom she had struck a blow, from the effects of which he had died. He should call Dr. Dorrian first, as he desired to get away to his patients, and would come on Thursday to be bound over if the prisoner was committed.

After repeating his former evidence, Dr. Dorrian said it was his belief that the wound would not be caused with a poker. A sharp instrument would have done it. It was an incised wound, and there was no fracture internal or external to the skull. It did not take a severe blow to produce the wound – Alderman Walmsley: If you had never heard anything of the means by which this wound had been caused, what conclusion would you have arrived at? – Mr. Dorrian: I should have considered that some slight blow from a sharp instrument had caused it. It did not require a heavy blow, and the spoon I have seen would produce it. The deceased told me that he was struck with a coal shovel. Ald. Walmsley: You cannot reconcile the wound with a blow from a poker? Mr. Dorrian: No, I should have expected more severe external injury. Mr. Hall: Would the edge of the spoon do it? Mr. Dorrian: The handle of the spoon struck on the head by a woman of prisoner's height on a person the height of deceased, who was small in stature, would have caused the wound, and two blows from the circular (bowl) end might have done it. Ald Walmsley: Are you of opinion that the spoon handle, wielded by a strong women like the prisoner, would have inflicted the wound: Mr. Dorrian: I have no doubt about it.

The witness Wilson said that prisoner struck deceased twice on the head, and repeated her former evidence, as did other witnesses (Whiteley, Ironfield, and

P.C. Austin), who were called. The police officer, in answer to prisoner, said that deceased did not return to the house after the blow, which she maintained he did. Prisoner, in answer to the usual question, said: I am sorry for hitting deceased with a spoon, and I was in a bad temper. He ran at me to shove me in the fire. I got hold of him, and he got hold of me and dragged me out. I had a spoon in my hand with which I had been stirring some broth. I struck him with a spoon outside, for he would not let me go. He would not let me go first time so I struck him a second time with a spoon. He let me go then, and fell down, and I turned into my house. When I went in I looked at the spoon and blood was upon it I said to myself, 'I am very sorry for he is an old lodger, but I cannot have hurt him much, for I struck him with the head part of the spoon.' He always liked me, and I given him his dinner many a time. He was very drunk. I cannot say now where he caught me when he was trying to put me in the fire. I am very sorry for it.

James Brown was called as a witness in her favour and repeated his statement that deceased returned to the house and said that prisoner had struck him on an old wound.

The magistrates then committed prisoner for trail at the Assizes.

A judge considers the facts of the case before him...

CROWN COURT – MONDAY.
(BEFORE SIR. JOHN MELLOR)
MANSLAUGHTER AT BOLTON

Ann Maddon, 56, was indicted for having at Bolton on the 25th June, feloniously killed and slain John Stewart. Mr Cottingham prosecuted; prisoner was not defended by counsel. The prisoner and deceased had been acquainted for some time prior to the night in question. Stewart had lodged at prisoner's house. On the night stated he went to prisoner's house, and an altercation took place between them. Prisoner seized a heavy iron spoon and stuck deceased on the head with it. She pushed him into the street, and she was there seen with a candle in one hand a piece of iron in the other, and with the latter she struck him several times on the head. Unfortunately she struck him on a part of the head where there was a wound which had been previously inflicted. Deceased was drunk at the time. Stewart was taken home and attended by a surgeon. Inflammation supervened, an abscess formed on the brain, and the unfortunate man died on the 22nd July. The jury found prisoner guilty, and his Lordship, taking into account the fact that she had been in prison three months, and taking into account the whole of the circumstance of the case, said he did not think he was showing too great leniency in sentencing her to six months imprisonment.

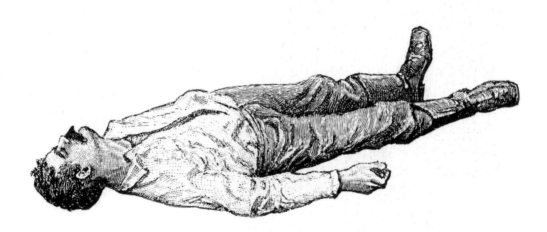

A murdered man lies where he fell...

TEN

'BEER AND POVERTY' - SHOCKING NEGLECT OF A CHILD, 1882

(FROM THE *JOURNAL*, SATURDAY 1 APRIL 1882)

An inquest into the cause of the death of an infant named Jane Ellen Whittle aged four months, daughter of James Whittle, spindle and fly forger, living at 8 Back Spring Street, Rose Hill, was held at the Uncle Tom's Cabin beer house, Lever Street, by Rowland Taylor, Esq., Borough Coroner, on Wednesday. Alice Whittle, mother of the deceased, said her husband had been working at Rochdale for about seven weeks, and she had received 32s. from him during the last three weeks to keep five of them at home. Previous to sending the money he came over, paid the rent, and bought the children clogs etc. The deceased was a delicate child at its birth, and a fortnight after it was born she commenced to feed it with bread and milk. On Thursday the 16th inst., one of the neighbours took deceased to the relieving officer whilst witness was next door, and he ordered its removal to the workhouse on Wednesday last, and it died on Sunday. She took the deceased to Dr. Dorrian on the 15th inst., and he told her to take to the infirmary, but it was too late to get a 'recommend.' A neighbour named Mrs. Spence had charge of deceased for two months whilst witness went to work. Mrs. Partington, who kept it a fortnight, but witness could not work after that, and had fed the child herself since. She had often 'done her work on a gill of beer', but had never been found drunk in the house by the neighbours. Mrs. Spence 70, Bridgman Street, said in November she went to live with Mrs Whittle, whose husband was at home

A ball and chain was often used to secure the prisoner in jail.

at that time. There were four children at that time, and one was born whilst she was living there. The deceased when born was 'as fine and healthy a child as she would wish to see.' She stayed at Mrs. Whittle's for about eight week, and nursed deceased the whole of that time. Mrs. Whittle went to work within three weeks of her confinement, and said she earned 11s. per week. Whilst witness was there the mother did her duty as far as she could to the child. After seeing the body of the deceased, witness said it was not half as big as when born. Ellen Partington, married woman, 10 Back Spring Street, said Mrs Whittle gave deceased to her to nurse about five or six weeks ago. She received 3s. 6d. the first week, and 3s. the week afterwards, and the mother then took the child away because she was out of work through an alternation in the machinery. The child was poorly, but improved during the time she had it. Mrs. Whittle was drunk three or four times a week, and when she went to the Queen Elizabeth 'to get the drink she left deceased on the bed, Mrs. Whittle had neglected the child very much to her knowledge.' She saw three men running Mrs Whittle about in a wheelbarrow on the day

Mrs. Hamer took deceased to the workhouse. Ann Hamer, married woman, 9, Back Spring Street, said the child was full-grown when born, and she had since seen Mrs Whittle drunk three or four times a week. In consequence at the general indignation of the neighbours she fetched deceased out of the house, where it was lying in a filthy condition, on the 16th inst. A bottle lay near the child, the contents of which were putrid, and appeared to be sugar and water. She took the baby to Dr. Mallett, who said it appeared to have been laid on, and it was afterwards taken to the workhouse, where it remained until fetched out by the mother. James Whittle, father of the deceased, said he had been working at Rochdale three months, and earned 20s. to 30s. per week. When he did not come home he sent his wife various amounts from 7s. to 15s. weekly. He was aware of his wife's drunken habits. Dr. Dorrian said he had known Mrs. Whittle 25 years. He knew that she had ruptured a blood vessel. He first saw the deceased child on the third of the month, when it was vaccinated, and had since seen it twice. On the latter occasion the mother said it had diarrhoea. He made an examination of deceased on Tuesday. There was no external injury but it was extremely emaciated. He had no hesitation in saying death was caused by mesenteric disease, and if it had improper food death would be accelerated. Under the most judicious treatment this disease often produced death in a town like Bolton. The surroundings of the case – beer and poverty, and all that – no doubt had a great deal to do with it. The child now weighed 5lb 3oz which was below the weight of an average child at birth. The Coroner remarked upon the gross abuse and neglect of the child by the mother, and said if he had his will he would commit the women for manslaughter. He hoped if they could not punish her the Guardians would take it up. The jury returned a verdict of death from 'Natural Causes', censured the mother, and urged the desirability of a prosecution by the Board of Guardians.

ELEVEN

THE KEARSLEY MURDER, 1883

(FROM THE *BOLTON EVENING NEWS*, MONDAY 12 FEBRUARY 1883)

EXECUTION OF ABRAHAM THOMAS AT STRANGEWAYS GAOL THIS MORNING.

The last dread scene in the fearful tragedy of Kearsley Moss was enacted this morning within the precincts of Strangeways Gaol, in the strictest privacy, the only witnesses of the execution of Abraham Thomas, the murderer of Mrs. Christiana Leigh, being the Deputy Sheriff (Mr. Woodcock), the Governor of the Gaol (Major Preston), the Rev. J. Brash, Wesleyan minister (who has attended Thomas since his condemnation), Dr. Braddon, surgeon of the prison, Dr. Kitchen, assistant surgeon, and one or two officials of the gaol.

This morning broke dull, raw and cold. The neighbourhood of the gaol presented a most uninviting aspect, a biting east wind prevailed, and the whole surroundings seemed to be in keeping with the scene inside the prison. The cheerlessness of the morning, however, did not prevent the gathering of nearly 500 persons – men, women, and even young children – who had assembled for the purpose of gratifying a morbid curiosity, so far as it could be satisfied, by the sight of the hoisting of the black flag. All eyes were directed towards the flagstaff for a quarter of an hour before the time fixed for the execution, eight o'clock.

A cell where a convict would be held.

The curiosity of the crowd previous to that time was divided by witnessing the persons passing from and entering the gaol, and watching the ominously convulsive swinging of the rope, from which the black signal of death was soon to be waving in the stiff morning breeze. Now comes a tiny girl with a jug of hot coffee and a parcel, evidently the breakfast of some unlucky wight incarcerated within the prison, and awaiting his trial. She knocks at the heavy ponderous wicket door and is admitted. The arrival of the Salford prison van is an event of some interest to the crowd. The vehicle drives up, the massive double doors are thrown back, and the van enters, to emerge again in a few minutes with its load of prisoners for examination before the Salford Bench. Even the advent of a milk-cart, with its daily supply for the gaol, is a circumstance which is taken some interest in by the crowd of sightseers. About twenty-five minutes to eight the Under Sheriff, Mr. Woodcock, arrived, the gaol surgeon, Dr. Braddon, also walks up, and is admitted. As early as seven o'clock the Rev. J. Brash arrived, and was conducted to the condemned cell. The patience of the crowd is at last rewarded by the appearance, at three minutes past eight, of the head and shoulders of a prison warder at the trap-door near the foot of the flagstaff, and this official commences to busy himself in hoisting the flag black and dismal, which is to announce to the waiting throng the fact of the violent death which has just taken place within the gaol. The flag is speedily drawn into position and commences flapping with the breeze. The throng gaze for a minute or two and then slowly disperse.

As we have intimated, the execution was witnessed only by those whose vocation calls upon them to perform the grim duty of being present at the final scene. The Governor of the Gaol (Major Preston) has however given the representatives of the Press who waited on him some details as to Thomas's last moments. Marwood, the executioner, arrived at the gaol on Friday night, but did not sleep in the prison before Sunday night. The condemned man rose this morning at six o'clock, having passed a pretty good night. The only breakfast he took was a cup of tea, refusing everything in the shape of solid food. The Rev. J. Brash, as we have stated, visited him at seven, and remained with him to the last. The culprit was resigned to his fate, and was very penitent. Indeed, ever since his condemnation his conduct has been most exemplary, always confessing his guilt and expressing his sorrow for the crime. He has been a daily attendant at service in the prison chapel, listening to the ministrations of the prison chaplain, the Rev. Mr. Dreaper, and on Sunday he attended the chapel twice. This morning, when visited by Marwood about a quarter to eight, for the pinioning process, Thomas seemed somewhat faint, but speedily recovering he walked to the scaffold without assistance, Marwood only holding him by one of his pinioned arms as the sad procession wended its way to the scaffold, the culprit meanwhile responding to the service recited by Mr. Brash. As the final words, 'Lord have mercy upon me' had left his lips, the cap was drawn over his face, the rope was adjusted, and stepping quickly back the executioner touched the spring catch which supports the drop, and the soul of the unhappy man was hurried to its Maker. The drop was one of 8ft, 6in., and the culprit died instantaneously, to use the Governor's expression, 'without even the twitter of a finger.' Previous to his death the culprit intimated to the Governor that he should like the books of a religious character which he had been perusing since his condemnation to be given to his sister, a dying wish which will, of course, be acceded to.

THE INQUEST

The formal inquisition on the body of Thomas was heard in the Warden's Reading-room, inside the prison, at a quarter to twelve o'clock, by Mr. Price, the district county coroner. None but the jury and representatives of the press were admitted. The jury, having been sworn, adjourned to view the body, which lay in the mortuary near the place of execution. The head of deceased was uncovered for inspection by the jury, but the neck was completely clothed; so that no trace of the mark made by the rope was visible. Deceased's countenance was placid, no contortion disfiguring the feature. The complexion and ears were rather livid, and latterly Thomas appears to have allowed his beard to grow slightly. His crisp, dark hair, gathered closely around his forehead, and beyond the blue hue of the face already mentioned, deceased might have been sleeping calmly. Near at hand was the fatal drop, and the hole dug out to receive his body was filled up, the mould being fresh on the top, whilst in one corner a few feet distant was the newly opened grave. The simple stone records at the spot where the three 'Manchester Martyrs' were interred were also in the immediate neighbourhood. On the return of the jury, Major Preston, governor of the prison, was called. He said: 'The dead body now shown to this inquest jury is that of Abraham Thomas. It is the identical body of the man of that name who was lately confined in this prison under sentence of death. I was present at the trial at the assizes, and heard the sentenced pronounced. I was present at eight o'clock this morning when judgement of death by hanging was duly carried into effect. The body remained hanging one hour, was then taken down and found to be dead by the surgeon of the prison. Deceased fell eight feet six inches when the bolt was drawn.

The Foreman of the jury (Mr. Thomas Lee): I should like to ask if the prisoner made the confession before he died, – Major Preston: He has never denied it from the beginning. He made no written confession.

Owing to the absence of the doctor some delay ensued at this point:- The Coroner said his only object was to ask the doctor what was the cause of death and whether it was instantaneous, but Major Preston might probably to able to speak to that:- Major Preston: Yes I can, He never moved – not a finger, – The Coroner:

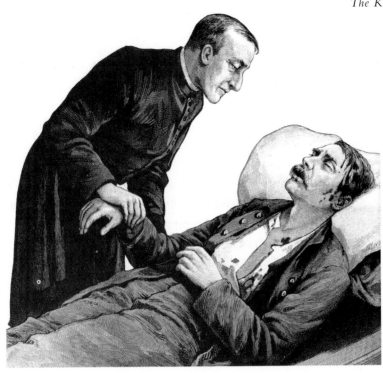

A doctor attends
to a dying victim.

And the cause of death; did you hear the doctor say whether it was dislocation of the neck or strangulation? – Major Preston; His neck was dislocated.

Mr. C.E.H. Kitchen, assistant surgeon to the prison, now arrived, and in answer to the Coroner said: I was present when sentence of death was carried into effect upon Abraham Thomas. I examined the body of deceased about half an hour after the execution, although it remained hanging the full hour. I found the body to be dead, and death was caused most probably from dislocation of the neck. Death was instantaneous – A Juror: Would the neck, being dislocated, have the effect of causing the dislocation about the ears? – Mr. Kitchen: I think it is merely the strangulation from the cord stopping the circulation.

The Coroner said that was all the evidence usually adduced on these cases. The duty of the jury now was to say whether the judgement of death had been duly carried into effect upon the deceased, in pursuance of the sentence passed upon him for the wilful murder of Christiana Leigh. He asked if such was their opinion? The jury replied in the affirmative.

The foreman desired to put a question to the representatives of the press, but the coroner refused permission, whereupon he asked Major Preston whether there being no representatives of the press present at the execution application had been made for admission. – The Coroner said application would be made through the Sheriff. – Major Preston said he told one or two reporters they could only obtain admission by order from the Sheriff.

The Foreman moved: 'That the reporters of the press in future make application to the Sheriff for admission to all executions in the gaol.' This having been seconded, another juror asked whether it was the unanimous opinion that the press would be admitted, and if so they must request the Coroner to communicate with the Sheriff to that effect? – Another juror said he thought such should be the case. – The Coroner said it was not altogether leaving the matter to one side in the sense of having it solely in the hands of the Sheriff, for the law prescribed that the inquest should be told. – One or two jurors dissented from the proposition on the ground that they had quite sufficient in the evidence of the doctor and governor upon which to arrive at the cause of death. – The Coroner on this said any expression of opinion, unless unanimous, would be nugatory in effect, whereupon the foreman withdrew his motion, the Coroner remarking that the reporters could make use of the information gained that day in making future applications. The proceedings then terminated.

THE CULPRIT'S DEMEANOUR

The demeanour of the condemned man during his incarceration, and up to the time of his execution, has presented no startling developments, and there is a confident belief on the part of his spiritual adviser, the Rev. John Brash, of the Gravel Lane Wesleyan Circuit, Manchester and minister of Sussex Street Chapel, that he died thoroughly penitent, and with a firm faith in Divine saving grace. The officials of the prison, and all who have been brought in contact with Thomas are most favourably impressed with the conduct. By his special request, the Rev. J. Brash first visited the convict on the 1st inst, and has been with him daily since that date, and latterly devoting two visits each day to the unfortunate criminal. As has been mentioned also, the Rev. Josiah Mee, of the Bridge Street Circuit, Bolton, interviewed Thomas on two occasions, the last being on Saturday, when he accompanied Mr. Brash. Throughout Thomas has tacitly admitted his guilt, and while making no written statement or formal confession, his attitude has been one of deep contrition and remorse, the latter emotion seeming to completely overpower him until the past week, when he brightened and assumed a hopeful cheerfulness, looking beyond the dreadful death which was soon to terminate his existence. His interviews with his relatives have been of the most affecting description, and he has been much concerned at the deep distress and misery into which they were thrown by his position. On Thursday last two sisters from Denbigh were admitted to the condemned cell; but since then he has only had converse with Mr. Brash. On Sunday he attended two services in the prison chapel, and that in the afternoon was of most appropriate character, the officiating clergyman taking for his text the prayer of the penitent thief, 'Lord, remember me when Thou comest into Thy Kingdom.' The emotion of the prisoners was almost universal, and the chaplain himself afterwards alluded to the deeply affecting character of the service. A young lady to whom Thomas was engaged had one interview with him last week. Mr. Brash left the convict about half-past nine on Sunday night, and he then appeared perfectly calm, collected, and resigned. His mind had never been disturbed by any hope of a reprieve, and as the fatal hour approached he appeared to regard his doom with decreasing dread. The minister arrived before seven this morning, and immediately proceeded to the cell. Thomas had then been up about an hour, was dressed in his own clothes, and had sent his breakfast away untested with the exception of a cup of tea. He met Mr Brash composedly, said he had passed a better night than of late, sleeping quietly for several hours. The rev. gentleman and the condemned mutually engaged in prayer, and on the arrival of Marwood he found them on their knees. The executioner lightly tapped the convict on his shoulder, and he rose at once, showing no sign of weakness or failing nerve. The pinioning process was rapidly effected. the prisoner at once placing his hands behind his back in the position requested by Marwood, and without a word walked firmly to the scaffold, Mr. Brash continuing to pray fervently, and accompanying Thomas to afford him needful support and consolation. The fatal drop reached, the cap was drawn over his eyes, his legs fastened, the spring drawn, and all was over. The minister, who was reading a few passages from the Liturgy, turned round surprised at the rapidity with which the law's last and most dread sentence had been carried out, and the body then hung motionless, without the movement of a muscle. Although very open with his spiritual adviser, Thomas was naturally a man of few words and appeared reticent when addressed by strangers. The Bible and Wesleyan hymn book were his constant companions after the conviction, together with other religious works supplied by his friends. He told Mr. Brash that he had suffered severely from brain fever about a year ago, and since that time the after effects of drink had had a maddening influence. He said had he been really

The assailant raised his pistol and took aim...

intoxicated he did not think he should have shot Mrs. Leigh, but it was during the morbid and overstrained condition of his mind, consequent upon too free indulgence, that he committed the act. He had never said one word against the deceased woman, or attempted to justify his crime by allusion to her conduct in the slightest degree, merely replying in answer to a question on the point, 'We did not get on very well together.'

Mr. Wm. Hooper, Lee Green, Kent, having appealed to the Home Secretary to order an inquiry into the state of mind of the convict, Abraham Thomas, received the following communication from Sir. William Harcourt: 'Pressing – Whitehall, Feb. 10, 1883 – Sir – In reply to your application in behalf of Abraham Thomas, now lying under sentence of death in Strangeways Prison, I am directed by the Secretary of State to acquaint you that, after a careful consideration of all the facts of this case, he has not felt justified in advising Her Majesty to interface with the due course of the law. – I am sir, your obedient servant, A.F, O. LIDDELL. – Mr. W.J. Hooper.'

TWELVE

ROBBERY WITH VIOLENCE AT BOLTON, 1884

(FROM THE *BOLTON JOURNAL*, SATURDAY 26 JANUARY 1884)

James McCarty, 27, factory operative and Mary Gibson, 21, factory operative, were charged with robbery with violence from the person of James Talbot, at Bolton, on the 27th December. Mr. Blair prosecuted, and prisoners were undefended. The case for the prosecution was that Talbot, who is a carter, living in Halliwell Road, went to the Founder's Arms, Ashburner Street, on the night of the 27th December, about half-past ten, when the prisoners, with other persons came in. They said they were without money and had come from Preston. He paid for a glass of ale each, and it was afterwards agreed that he should go home with the prisoners to supper, and he was to find the 'allowance.' They went together down Spring Gardens and into Back Spring Gardens, and in the darkness the two women who were present crossed their legs and threw him to the ground. McCarty seized him by the throat and kicked him about the ribs. A woman who escaped put her hand into his pocket and robbed him of a half -a-crown, a two shilling piece and some coppers. He cried out 'murder' and P.C. Tootill coming up he put the prisoners into custody. Talbot stuck to Gibson, and McCarty was close by. Another woman was charged before the magistrates but prosecutor could not identify her, and she was dismissed. McCarty said he came from Manchester, and had a ticket for Blackburn. Why he got out at Bolton, and what he did there he could not remember. Gibson had no defence, and his lordship having summed up, the jury returned a verdict of 'guilty' against both prisoners, who each acknowledged former convictions for felony. Previous to sentence, McCarty said he only came out of prison, after serving eighteen months on the day of the offence, and he got too much drink. The judge said McCarty was too dangerous a character to be at large, and he would not be doing his duty if he sentenced him to any less than five years penal servitude. Gibson was sent to prison for twelve months hard labour.

DOUBLE EXECUTION AT STRANGEWAYS, 1884

(FROM THE *BOLTON EVENING NEWS*, MONDAY 24 NOVEMBER 1884)

CONFESSIONS OF KAY HOWARTH AND HENRY HAMMOND SWINDELLS

Within the gloomy walls of Strangeways Gaol, Manchester, this morning Kay Howarth, the murderer of Richard Lee Dugdale, at Bolton, and Henry Hammond Swindells, for the murder of James Wild, at Oldham, paid the death penalties for their awful crimes. The wonderful, and at the same time indisputable train of circumstances which connected Howarth with the murder, enclosing him, as it were with a chain of evidence from which there was no escape, precluded from the first day idea of a reprieve, notwithstanding his own unaccountable, if not impious declaration of innocence. On the other hand Swindells and his friends had hope of a reprieve, which, however, has not been granted. Therefore, the usual three Sundays which by law are allowed to transpire between the passing of the sentence and its dread fulfilment having elapsed, Howarth and Swindells this morning died at the hands of the common hangman.

The appearance of the vicinity of the gaol was dreary in the extreme, the thick fog hanging over all like a funeral pall, making all dark and dismal. In the semi-darkness the prison, with its high walls, loomed out ugly enough. The

Two prisoners sit in chains.

passers by went to and fro to their ordinary avocations, seemingly careless as to the fate of the two men confined within those prison walls. Beyond the Press men no one had journeyed specially to be witnesses of the last act, so far as it is given to the public to use, of the tragedy which has excited interest of so many townspeople. And there was nothing to be seen by the spectator, however eager or curious he might be, for, of course, only the representatives of the Press were given admittance to the gaol. Among the few that did linger near the portals of the gaol, the exciting question was as to whether a reprieve had been received for Swindells. This the reporters who were waiting for the time when they would be allowed to enter the gaol, were able to ascertain definitely, for shortly before seven o'clock they were officially informed that the Home Secretary in his last communication had definitely refused to grant a respite, and that, therefore, the fate of Swindells as well as that of Howarth was sealed. As the morning progressed stragglers swelled the number of the curious who stood waiting for the signal that the dread sentence of the law had been executed, and at about a quarter to eight o'clock there were about 50 or 60 persons present. Naturally from this time until eight o'clock the interest increased as to the event which was in progress within the gaol. Every cab that rolled up the street was keenly scrutinised, and the appearance of the Under Sheriff (Mr. Costeker) led to another speculation as to whether a reprieve had arrived. But a few minutes more sufficed to place all doubt at rest, for at exactly one minute past eight o'clock the black signal, announcing the ushering of the two condemned men into eternity, was seen hoisted on the flagstaff of the prison. All was over so far as the spectators were concerned, and the group rapidly dispersed, each to go on his way, no doubt, with a vivid impression of, and varied feelings respecting, the fate of those who had expiated their crime upon the scaffold. Still one remained, a woman, with a shawl over her head, who had previously walked about the street in a restless manner, evidently by her grief-stricken and disturbed appearance having some connection with the unhappy men. As the certainty of the penalty having been inflicted came to her mind she fell down on the flags in a violent fit of weeping, bewailing the untimely end of him for whom she mourned.

THE SCAFFOLD SCENE

In accordance with previous arrangements a limited number of representatives of the press were admitted at the gaol at a quarter to eight. They were conducted into the warden's lodge at the entrance to the prison to await the arrival of the Governor, Major Preston, who appeared at five minutes to eight o'clock and examined the credentials in the possession of the reporters enabling them to be present at the executions. These being considered satisfactory, they were conducted by a warder across the prison yard to the space at front of the scaffold. The dread instrument of death is fixed in the usual place facing the back of the Assize Courts, but which is not observable from any part of the prison in the yard, being enclosed by high walls. At the moment of the arrival of the reporters and the warden the executioner, Berry, of Bradford, and his assistant were on the scaffold completing the final arrangements on the drop. The ropes were left hanging from the cross beam whilst they retired to the interior of the prison. At a minute and a half past eight o'clock the sound of the voice of the prison chaplain, the Rev. J. Dreaper, could be heard in the distance, as the dread cortege approached, intoning the burial service of the Church of England. Presently that gentleman appeared, clad in his surplice, and followed by Mr. William Cox, town missionary of Oldham, also attired in a surplice. Mr. Dreaper has been in attendance on Howarth since his condemnation, and Mr. Cox, has been giving spiritual consolation to Swindells. Following the two ministers were the condemned men, Howarth came first led by Berry, the executioner, and Swindells followed, accompanied by the hangman's assistant. Howarth was attired in a black coat and vest and light pair of trousers, whilst Swindells was dressed in a black suit. The demeanour of the two men was striking by the force of contrast. Swindells was deadly pale, but very firm. He had his hands clasped over his breast, as in the attitude of prayer, and his eyes were closed. He kept repeating after the Home Missionary the responses in the service, such as, 'Lord have mercy upon me.' 'Oh, Lord receive my soul,' his first utterance as he appeared on the scaffold being 'I thank Thee that thou art my Saviour.' The demeanour of Kay Howarth on the other hand was pitiable in the extreme. He cried and wept aloud, ejaculating repeatedly 'Oh Lord, Oh Lord,' in the most abject misery and fear. Those who were present in the Assize Courts on the afternoon and evening of his trial will have some idea as to his condition. As then his face was greatly flushed, the perspiration exuding from very pore, and in addition, as we have said, he kept exclaiming, 'Oh, Lord!' Both male-factors were

James Berry, executioner.

pinioned when they appeared on the scaffold, and each had their hands together, Howarth's being placed one on the other. The ropes were placed simultaneously on the heads of the two condemned, Howarth assisting by moving his head from side to side, and this was followed by the adjustment of the white caps. Just as Berry was pulling the cap on the head of Howarth, he exclaimed, 'Oh, Lord, help me!' and Swindells, as the same operation was being performed, said, 'Oh, Lord, receive my soul.' Precisely at 3½ minutes past eight Berry, the executioner, stepped back along with his assistant, leaving the two men standing alone on the fatal drop. The lever was then released, the deep fall, and the men descended with a painful thud. It was evident to the onlookers that death was doubly instantaneous. Not the slightest movement was visible in any part of the bodies, and were the position of the hands remained unchanged, not the least motion being observable. The bodies swung in the air amid a silence which might be felt, and all was over.

Returning to the immediate chain of circumstances which proceeded the final scene, we may state that the executioner, Berry, arrived in Manchester on Saturday, and slept in the city the night, but on Sunday night he slept in the gaol. Both the condemned men rose about two minutes to six o'clock this morning, and having washed and dressed themselves they partook of a breakfast of bread and butter and tea, Howarth, eating freely, but Swindells rather sparingly. About 20 minutes past six the Rev. J. Dreaper repaired to the cell of Howarth and Mr. Cox to that of Swindells, both gentlemen remaining with them to the close. At four minutes to eight Berry visited the cells of each and performed the operation of pinioning, and there the procession was formed to the scaffold, led up by the chaplain and missionary; then followed the two condemned men, and the chief warden, deputy chief warden, the two medical men, Dr. Braddon and Dr. Paton, and the Under Sheriff (Mr. Costeker) bringing up the rear. The rope used for Swindells was a new one, but the one employed in the case of Howarth has been used on four similar occasions previously. The length of drop was eight feet.

A considerable group of people hung around the prison after the execution, some of whom were evidently waiting for discharged prisoners. At nine o'clock the black flag was slowly hauled down; at the same time as the bodies of the murderers were removed to the mortuary. Mr. Cox left the prison between eight and nine, and on being interviewed he said the culprit Swindells had confessed his crime, but refused to give the substance of a statement. Berry, the executioner, also left quietly, and after calling at a neighbouring hotel, departed by train. Berry was very reticent, simply remarking in answer to question, that the men died without a quiver, instantaneously.

THE INQUEST

On the bodies of Howarth and Swindells was opened at seven o'clock, in the library of the prison, before Mr. F. Price, district coroner. After being sworn, the jury was taken to the mortuary to view the bodies, passing on their way the single open grave which both men are now interred, dug in an angle of the wall, the initial names and the dates of execution of several other murderers being visible on white bricks set in the wall. Amongst the more recent of these was that of Abraham Thomas, executed for the Kearsley murder. A little further to the right was the place slabs, dressed in ordinary attire. Swindells was the first to come under notice on entering the mortuary, and he presented the calm appearance of sleep, except perhaps that the face wore the wax-like pallor of death. There were no evidence of the slightest agitation. The eyes closed naturally. Howarth on the other hand, was a very different spectacle. His face was pale but livid, haged with purple, the ears and lips being of an exceedingly pronounced purple hue. Blood had dried around the nostrils, as if the shock had caused a sudden haemorrhage at the nose, and the culprit had also apparently bitten his tongue, as there were traces of blood round the mouth. The eyes are partially open and glazed, and the body, even at the short interval of three hours from death, had swollen considerably. The neck appeared to be completely broken, but there was very little to indicate the presence of the fatal rope, beyond an abnormal thickness of the lower part of the throat and one discolouration. Howarth was dressed in a black coat and waistcoat and light fawn trousers, his boots being well polished.

The jury having returned from their ghastly task of viewing the bodies, the Coroner intimated that he would take the case of Swindells first, remarking that the evidence to be tendered was that usual in all cases of this description, and simply formal.

Major J. W. Preston, governor of her Majesty's prison, Cheetham, was then sworn, and his formal prepared statement read over by the Coroner, to the effect that the body which the jury had been shown as that of Henry Hammond Swindells was that of the identical man who was sentenced to death. On the 18th July he was committed by one of the coroners for the county, and on the 14th August by the magistrates of Oldham, to take his trial for the wilful murder of James Wild. Accordingly at the last assizes for the county he was indicted, tried, and convicted, and sentenced to be hanged by the neck until he was dead. He (witness) was present this morning at eight o'clock when the sentence of death by hanging was duly carried into effect within the walls of the prison. The body of the deceased remained hanging one hour, when it was taken down and found to be dead. It was examined by the assistant surgeon. There was no deviation in this case from the trial method of hanging prisoners to death which was carried into effect by an executioner appointed by the Sheriff.

In answer to the Coroner it was stated that the culprit was a committed clerk and that he had passed his 52nd birthday whilst in prison.

The Coroner: He fell a distance of what?

Major Preston: Eight feet.

The Coroner asked the jury if they desired to question Major Preston. Sometimes, he said, the question had been put whether there were any members of the Press present at the execution. That question might be asked now.

A Juror: Did the prisoner make any confession?

Major Preston: I have been informed that he made a confession to a minister of his guilt.

Mr. J Cox of Oldham, said that was so.

A Juror: Were any members of the Press at the execution?

Major Preston: There were four.

Mr. R. N. Paton, assistant surgeon of the prison, said he was present at eight o'clock this morning when sentence of death was carried into effect. He examined the body about two hours and a half afterwards, and found it to be dead. Death was caused, in his opinion, by injury to the spinal chord produced by fracture of the upper cervical vertebrae, the results of hanging

The Coroner: Was death instantaneous in your opinion?

Witness: It was.

A Juror: It not a usual thing to examine the body one hour after hanging?

Witness: I satisfied myself he was dead before I left him after the execution, and I examined the body again after it was taken down.

This was the whole of the evidence, and the Coroner, briefly directed the jury that they had to find whether the body they had viewed was that of Swindells sentenced to death, and that the judgment had been executed according to law.

A juror wished to know whether any reporter was present at the execution who was also present at the trial when Swindells was sentenced to death.

Major Preston could not say. He himself was present on both occasions.

The Juror said he thought it would be more satisfactory to the public if a reporter who was present at the passing of sentence was also present at the execution.

The Foreman said Major Preston was there, and they could take his word.

The Coroner said the friends of the deceased were accorded permission to be present if they chose, but it was very rarely they availed themselves of it.

A formal verdict that Swindells died by hanging in accordance with the sentence of the Court was then returned.

The evidence in this crime of the Bolton murderer, Howarth – was previously similar, – Major Preston he passed as the sentence and execution. He remained hanging for one hour and was 25 years of age, the drop eight feet.

A Juror: Did he make any confession?

Bolton Old Courts.

Major Preston: He confessed to the chaplain Mr. Dreaper.

The Coroner: The same answer as to gentleman of the Press being present will apply here?

Major Preston: Yes sir.

Dr. Paton also gave similar evidence to that in the last case.

A Juror: Was death instantaneous in your opinion?

Witness: It was.

A Juror: Did the executioner carry out his duties with entire satisfaction? There were no complaints?

Witness: Everything was carried quite satisfactorily.

The Foreman: Have you facility to examine the body after death to see if a struggle has taken place?

Witness: Oh, yes we go down.

The Foreman: It's a kind of hole they drop into, isn't it?

Witness: Can we walk underneath the drop?

The Coroner: There was no struggle, I believe?

Witness: None.

A formal verdict to the effect that the sentence had been duly executed was then returned, and the proceedings terminated. The curious and morbidly inclined were still to be found in the precincts of the prison, but these slowly dispersed when the coroner's jury left the prison, and the melancholy tragedy was at an end, save for the interment of the bodies, which took place shortly afterwards.

THE CONFESSION

Last night, at nine o'clock, the Governor of the Gaol (Major Preston) had conversions with both the condemned men. Swindells said that he did not commit the murder of Wild knowingly. Howarth stated, 'I did not do it, and I would not die with a lie on my lips.' Howarth went to bed at seven o'clock, and seemed to sleep soundly; but Swindells sat reading the Bible and praying until three o'clock. He then went to bed, but was extremely restless. This morning, however, after being told that there was no reprieve, Swindells said, 'I went to the place with the intention of shooting the man, and I admit the justice of my sentence.' Howarth also admitted the justice of his sentence and has left a written confession with Mr. Dreaper, which is kept a profound secret. It will be forwarded to the Home Secretary. We understand that the substance of the confession is that he wilfully murdered Mr Dugdale and pillaged the body. The confession was scribbled on a sheet of notepaper. After praying for some time both men said they were sorry for what they had done, and hoped their repentance would be accepted.

THE FINAL INTERVIEWS

As stated below since his sentence Kay Howarth has been visited on several occasions by his relatives and friends. His father, however, has only seen him once, when the interview was of such a painful nature to the father that he has not sought another. The condemned man was a member of a family of 14 brothers and sisters, who are all living. Consequently they have not all been able to be present at one interview, but the older ones have visited him two or three together, as they have obtained permission, so that he has seen most of his brothers and sisters. He has received them in a self-controlled manner, expressing himself glad to see them and assuring them of his innocence of the crime for which he had suffered the extreme penalty of the law. His eldest sister, Mrs. Entwisle, has seen him several times, both before and after the trial, and besought him to acknowledge his guilt if he had committed the deed laid to his charge. He has, however, persistently maintained that he was innocent, and this he still reiterated to her at the final interview which took place on Saturday afternoon. Mrs. Entwisle was accompanied by two brothers, the older one and the other the next younger to the condemned man. They were admitted into the gaol about five o'clock and conducted to the presence of their brother in the cell where he has been confined since his doom was pronounced. A warder was present, but was careful not to interfere whilst they bid the convict farewell, for it was only a quarter of an hour. Under the sad circumstances they had little to say to each other. Each were deeply moved, but of the four the man whose end was so near was the calmest, and apparently prepared to meet his fate in the same determined spirit he has displayed since his apprehension. His brothers and sister are naturally reticent as to what passed between them, and no doubt they will have the sympathy of many in the painful position they have been placed, but we are able to state that he still as strongly as ever asserted that he was not the cause of Dugdale's terrible death. His family, therefore, had the hope, though the evidence would not appear to admit of the slightest, that possibly the law had erred, whilst they admitted that the sentence is apparently just. The confession of the murdered had now set the matter at rest, and they will have the consolation at any rate that he did not pass away with a lie upon his lips. Previous to the interview with his nearest relatives, and which was the last he had with anyone not connected with the prison, he was visited by one of his aunts, another aunt, who had not obtained the requisite permit, having to remain outside the prison gates. This interview took place about noon, and the parting between Howarth and his aunt was most affecting. Shortly afterwards Howarth had to undergo a more trying leave-taking, for he was seen by his uncle, a Mr. Trainor, of Lyon Street, who was accompanied by his wife and daughter, and the young woman to whom Howarth was engaged to be married.

Not a word was said as to the crime, the conversation having regard principally to the coming end of Howarth. Howarth looked much older for the terrible days he has spent in the condemned cell, and his beard having grown somewhat intensified the change in his appearance. This was noted by his visitors during their brief stay with him. When the last moment came, Howarth's sweetheart, spite of all that has been said that she had determined to forget him, completely broke down, her feelings of affection overcoming her. Tears were in the eyes of the convict as he took her hand for the last time and listened to her words of comfort and hope for the future. Indeed, the cheeks of all the party were wet with tears as they left the cell. The authorities of the prison say that it is a long time since a condemned man had as many visitors as Howarth did. Mr. Trainor, uncle of Howarth, has received a letter from him wholly devoted to the subject of the disposal of his property. He leaves his gold watch to his sweetheart (Miss Nabbs) which makes three watches she received from him, but one of these, a silver one, Howarth desires her to give to his cousin John, son of Mr. Trainor. The gold chain attached to the watch also became the property of Miss Nabbs, and moreover she has the choice of any other articles are left by him. The clothes and his few other articles are left to Mr. Trainor, the uncle, while several nieces and another sister are left a few dollar pieces to make broaches of. The sister is to have whatever her uncle chooses to give her. Mr. Trainor has had frequent letters from him, but in none was any allusion made to the crime. Miss Nabbs, who denies that statement that she had said anything wrong about Howarth with regard to his American career, did receive from Howarth during his stay in that country £11 in money, wherewith to purchase a ticket for her passage out, where she was to be married to him. So far had proceedings gone in this matter that the ticket was secured, and further the wedding ring was purchased, but due to a misunderstanding Miss Nabbs did not take the opportunity of proceeding to America. However, on Howarth's return to this country, the engagement between them was re-aroused and we have previously stated, she was with him on the night previous to the murder.

THE STORY OF THE CRIME

Is soon told. There was no complicated problems apparently no preconceived intent. Howarth was hard up, Dugdale was drunk and had money; what easier

Bradshawgate, *c.* 1902. (Image courtesy of Chris Driver)

than to walk him on to the waste ground, destroy with death-dealing wounds, and escape with the plunder. On the morning of the 3rd October, Mr Richard Lee Dugdale, a traveller in the employ of Messer's Austin Bros, brewers, Castleford, commenced his round in the Bolton district, his first transaction apparently being the receipt of a cheque for £8 from the landlord of the Greyhound Inn, Manchester Road. Thence he appears to have gone to the Fleece Hotel, Bradshawgate, arriving there about half-past ten, where he expected to meet Mr. Joseph Sharman, brewer, who, however, was not there. About eleven o'clock an acquaintance turned up in the person of Robert Hall, an Eagley oil merchant, who also done something in the beer trade. Dugdale and Hall was in conversion when Kay Howarth arrived on the scene. His appearance was pretty well known, but a descriptive line or two may be interesting. He was a muscular, straight-built, dark fellow, of about 25 rather good-looking than otherwise; though possessing a pair of shifty eyes. A black drooping moustache added to his appearance, but the lower jaw was too

Mawdsley Street – this view is from Bold Street looking south-west towards the Old Courts.

heavy from a physiological point of view, the eyes too closely set, and the forehead too narrow. In fact there was more animal than intellect in Howarth's countenance. He was a borer by trade, and had been some years in America, where from letters received since, he worked steadily in a Philadelphia foundry for a time, but left on winning a sum of 100 dollars in a gambling transaction, expressing the intention not to work again. From that time his career appears to have been that of a loafer – at any rate a downward one. He 'sponged' on acquaintances, and, it is alleged, resorted to fallacious purpose 'to raise the wind.' It thrown a lurid light on the crime he had committed that during the last week he has written a letter from Strangeways Gaol in which he says 'whilst in the United States about three years ago I was charged with a similar crime, but managed to get out of it.' Whether Philadelphia got too hot to hold him we know not, but he returned to England, and subsequently to Bolton about two months before the murder in an impecunious condition. He did not take up his abode with his parents, but lodged with Mrs. Williams in Haworth Street. This was the man who, unhappily for the unfortunate Dugdale, turned into the Fleece on the morning of the 3rd October. He was acquainted with Hall, who gave him an introduction to his victim. The usual free masonry of the bar-room was brought into play, Howarth was invited to drink, and the party were quickly in a fair way for having a convivial day. It is needless to trace their peregrinations from one public house to another. It will be remembered that Howarth throughout drank at his companions expense; and even when he lost a wager of 'drinks round' in a slugging contest, Hall paid the 'shot.' Howarth paid for his meal at Walker's restaurant out of a 2s. piece, greater portion of the day having been spent at the Fleece, where during the afternoon Howarth had a slight fracas with a man over a game of dominoes; an adjournment was made about six o'clock to the Crown and Cushion, Mealhouse Lane. At this time Dugdale was intoxicated, and his prisoner also apparently slightly under the influence of the day's potations. They were refused drink at this house, where Hall stayed to transact some business, and Howarth left arm in arm with Dugdale ostensibly to take him to the Wheat Sheaf Inn, where he was staying. Overwhelming evidence indicates that the Wheat Sheaf was never reached, not even approached. The attention of Mr. Arthur Smethurst was attracted in Bradshawgate by the appearance of the two men, Dugdale being so very drunk that he leant heavily on his companion for support. This was about seven o'clock, when they were in the vicinity of Silverwell Lane, Silverwell Street, and the Post Office. Three young girls saw Howarth and Dugdale with their arms around each other, the latter being unable to walk equably, proceed down Silverwell Street. At the corner of Messer's Hasler's warehouse Dugdale was observed to attempt to turn in the direction of the Parish Church, but Howarth forced him in the other direction to the waste land. From this point Dugdale was dead to the outside world. No eyes beheld him in this life but those of this murderer. The dread scene enacted at the back of Mr. Goodearll's premises can only be imagined. The pale October moon shone fully, now bright, now obscured by scurrying clouds. Whether it was in comparative light that the unhappy Dugdale took his last look at earthly surroundings; or whether the black curtain of cloud added, if such were possible, horror to that ghastly deed we know not. Whether the half-stupefied victim pleaded with his erstwhile boon companion, now his implacable destroyer, for the mercy which was so crudely denied we know not. Whether the first blow rendered him unconscious; or whether he struggled feebly as wound after wound, slash after slash, drained his life blood, until he gradually sank into oblivion, we know not. All we know is that at nine o'clock the rifled body was found lying face upwards, the features distorted by contusions, the neck mercilessly gashed and clasped in the right hand, the clothing disturbed, and the pockets empty but for a few coppers. An hour before this horrible discovery was made Howarth had called at the Fleece and enquired for Robert Hall, whom he subsequently found at the Crown and Cushion. Howarth was suddenly flush of money. He drank brandy, ordered it as freely for the company. His explanation to Hall as to the whereabouts of Dugdale was lame and contradictory. First, he had said left him at the Balmoral Hotel, and on being further pressed, that they had had words, and that he left him near the Mawdsley Street Chapel, going towards the Wheat Sheaf. After this we find Howarth in the front seats at the Theatre, joining his fellow lodgers in the side boxes, criticising the play, explaining the bruised and swollen condition of his hands, which were clean, but saying he had been 'letting a man have it right and left' over a quarrel at dominoes, and boastfully displaying a handful of gold. After the play there is more drinking, Howarth being free with his money, and ultimately returning to his lodgings and retiring to rest. Meantime Dugdale's body is conveyed to the Mortuary, School Hill, by the police, unknown and unidentified. The first impression is that a suicide has been committed. The police in the absence of any clue foster the idea and for a brief period it is supported by the presence of the knife in the dead man's hand, and some ragged writing in his pocket book, which as far as it was decipherable, was to the effect that he had done it though unsound mind, and bidding good-bye to all. The most casual examination however, was sufficient to convince that this strange entry was not in the hand writing of the man who would never hold a pencil again. When the excitement subsided the minor injuries came under notice, and, identification having been established between ten and eleven by the landlord of the Fleece and Mr. Sharman, doubts were dissolved in the certainty that a foul murder had been committed. From this point the Bolton borough police exhibited extraordinary activity. Hall was brought from Eagley, and by five o'clock Howarth was under arrest. In his posession was found the cheque paid to Dugdale, over £30 in gold, the dead man's watch and chain, as well as papers and documents belonging to him. Subsequent examination proved that the whole literally reeks with the damning evidence of blood. Blood on Howarth's clothes, blood on the money, blood on the watch and chain. And to account for all a single blow struck in a public-house dominoes brawl. On Saturday morning the 8th Howarth was brought before the Borough Magistrates and remanded. On the following Monday he was fully committed for trial at the Assizes by the justice's and coroner's jury. Possession of the murdered man's property was accounted for. Howarth in the following statement to the committing magistrate;- 'He and I stroll out of the Crown and Cushion together, I didn't notice the time.' 'We went up Mawdsley Street.' 'On the way he fell down'. 'He got up himself.' He said. 'I think we are not drunk.' 'We walked further up Mawdsley Street Chapel and stood there'. He said. 'I am going home where are you going to?' He said. 'I am going back to Bob Hall again, to the Crown and Cushion now.' He said. 'Be careful, don't get picked up now.' He said. 'What do you mean?' 'I said, if you get down you'll get robbed, that's what I mean.' He said. 'No, I won't; I'll give them to you before I'll have them stolen.' So he handed them to me, and I said, 'I will give them back to you at the Crown and Cushion, when we meet Bob Hall.' 'So I said,' 'So here and be there.' 'That's all that said.' Just a month a day after the murder Howarth stood in the dock at the Manchester Assizes Courts, before Mr. Justice Smith and a jury of the countrymen, sworn to try him on a charge involving life or death. The event is so recent, and the last in process in the minds of the public, that recognition is unnecessary. The trial was one of the greatest of murder assassinations, locally. The court was literally bulged by the general public including a large crowd from Bolton, and throughout the weary eleven hours that the ghastly details of the atrocious crime occupied in telling, and re-telling, interest and excitement never flagged. The culprit was perhaps outwardly amongst the most calm. All day and evening he sat in the dock listening with unclenched attitude to the tale of blood, occasionally consulting with his counsel, and general behaving as an interested outsider rather than as a man whose life hung by a thread. Mr. M. Fielding, solicitor, who was instructed in the interests of the prisoner, had made indefatigable efforts to secure his acquittal, but he was met by the fatal fact that whereas the evidence against him was deadly circumstantial, there was nothing to array against it. The only chance left was to discredit the story for the prosecution and to this and Mr. Cottingham, the counsel engaged, laboured with, for the prisoner, most unsatisfactory results. When the judge summed up in clear incisive terms, when the glamour of the defending counsel's rhetoric was stripped away, and the naked facts were revealed in vital succession, the general opinion anticipated the ultimate verdict. It was felt that Howarth's fate was sealed, and deservedly so, and such proved to be the case. Fifteen minutes sufficed for the jury, and they returned with the portentous word 'guilty' on the lips of the foreman. Even now Howarth's nerve was marvellous, and he listened composedly to the impressive pronouncement of the death

Mawdsley Street. (Courtesy of the *Bolton Evening News*)

sentence, his only utterance a brief protestation of innocence. He left the dock and descended the steps which shut him out eternally from the world, the echo of the 'Amen' still ringing through the court on the Judge's prayer for mercy for the miserable offender against the law of God and man. For twenty days he was an inmate of the condemned cell, visited occasionally by near relatives, his demeanour only increasing in quiet and reserve as the morn approached on which at the hands of the public executioners he has been launched into the great unknown. It may be well to add that the victim of the crime for which Howarth this morning paid the penalty, was 37 years of age, and resided with his wife and family of six young children at Belle Vue, Wakefield. After the inquest his body

Bradshawgate, looking towards the Shipgate entrance.

was interred in a family grave at Burnley Cemetery. Mrs. Dugdale and her orphaned family being left totally unprovided for a submission list for their benefit has been open in Bolton for some time past.

It may be interesting to add that since his conviction Howarth has conducted himself with the greatest fortitude, and was not afraid of speaking about his coming end. So recently as Friday last it is said that he remarked to a warder, who had observed that his time was getting short, that 'if it has to be, the sooner the better.' This conversion took place whilst Howarth had temporarily ceased to read one of the books with which he had been supplied. Before his trial newspapers as well as books were at Howarth's disposal, but after his sentence newspapers were prohibited. As we have previously stated he did not at first take kindly to the prison fare, but afterwards he ate heartily. He slept well and the prison officials concur in the opinion that he was one of the coolest criminals that ever occupied the condemned cell.

THE OLDHAM MURDER

Henry Hammond Swindells, who this morning was also despatched by the public executioner in Strangeways Gaol, was 51 years of age, and described as a clerk. The crime for which he suffered was the wilful murder of James Wild, at Oldham, on July 16th 1883. At the Manchester Assizes, where sentence was passed, he was further indicted with shooting at his wife, Susannah P. Swindells, with intent to murder her, but this count was not proceeded with on his conviction on the capital charge. The facts of the case were briefly as follow. The prisoner formerly resided at Oldham, and was married to the sister-in-law of the deceased. He had not lived happily with his wife, and had been separated from her. He went to America and stayed there some time, but on the 16th July, 1883, he appeared at his wife's house and asked her to live with him again. She refused, and he asked her to give him a saloon pistol there was in the house. This she declined to do, and their daughter becoming alarmed, went and fetched her uncle. What followed was not clear beyond a certain point. A witness saw Wild leaning on Swindells with his hand on the prisoner's collar. Immediately afterwards a pistol went off, and Wild staggered and fell. Prisoner was seen to fire at his wife. It was found that six bullets had been fired, and from a box brought by the prisoner from America six cartridges were missed. Wild's death was instantaneous. Swindells disappeared, and was not apprehended until August of the present year, when he said he would leave his defence to his solicitor. For the defence, counsel urged that there was no evidence that the prisoner had a pistol on the day in question, and even assuming that he had, it might accidentally have gone off during a struggle. Witnesses were called who gave the prisoner a good character. The jury, after an hour's consideration, found the prisoner 'Guilty.' Asked whether he had anything to say, the prisoner asserted his innocence, and thanked the Court for the patience and consideration they had bestowed on the case. He was resigned to meet his fate, but was as innocent as he could possible be. The learned Judge, in passing sentence of death, said he did not see how the jury could have given any other verdict. It will be in the minds of our readers that after this conviction Swindells made a written statement to the effect that the pistol exploded inadvertently whilst struggling with his wife and Wild, and that he had no murderer's intent. A petition to the Home Secretary for the commutation of his sentence was signed by 2,000 persons.

FOURTEEN

SHOCKING DISCOVERY ON CHORLEY OLD ROAD – PARTS OF A BODY FOUND, 1884

(FROM THE *BOLTON JOURNAL*, SATURDAY 31 MAY 1884)

HALLIWELL – PARTS OF BODY FOUND – LOST BY A MEDICAL STUDENT

On Tuesday night, about half-past six o'clock discovery of a most alarming nature was made on Chorley Old Road, Halliwell, the result of which was that the entire neighbourhood between the Victory and the Cocker was thrown into a state of great excitement. Mr. John Parker, foreman joiner, and tenant of the house situated at the entrance of the grounds above Halliwell Hall, belonging to T.H. Rushton, Esq., J.P., was in the plantation adjoining the house, when he noticed in the grass a brown paper parcel, picking it up he found it contained a portion of a woman's right arm, tightly bandaged with some old rags. The arm has been apparently severed a little above the elbow, but below this the hand and arm was perfect, the long fingers and general appearance left no doubt in the mind that it was the limb of a woman. At a very short distance from the same spot Mr. Parker also discovered a second parcel which contained a portion of a human skull. No part of the front or upper portion of the head was present, but the back section of the skull had appeared been sawn asunder with some fine instrument. Mr. Rushton was acquainted with the discovery, the police were communicated with P.C. Fitton of the county constabulary, taking possession of the remains. By this time, as may be supposed the affair had became noised abroad, and a woman called Flitcroft, living in St. Thomas Street, Brownlow Fold volunteered a statement. On Sunday, she says, past the plantation, along with her husband and son, they found a parcel near the spot indicated. The son was about to secure it, but the mother thinking it were blankets or other clothing, told him to leave them where they were. They proceeded home, and nothing more was thought of the discovery. On Tuesday night, however, the boy returned to the plantation, and secured a apron which he took and gave his mother, saying he had brought the present, at the same time telling her that he had in the parcel what looked like the arm of a women, on the advice of the mother, however, the lad returned the apron to the place where he had picked it up. The woman was narrating this story she noticed to be near them, and he was called into the house. On pointing out the locality where he stated he had found the apron, Mr. Parker made a fourth discovery, a quantity of a man's underclothing. All the said were taken possession of by P.C. Fitton and moved to the County Police Station. Supt. Holt directed the remains to be taken to the surgery of Mackie, St. Georges Road, and on being submitted to that gentleman he at once unravelled the apron. From the appearance of the bones he immediately came to the conclusion that they been practiced upon by some medical student, it appears to be the habit among some energetic enthusiastic students, the bones had apparently been moved from some medical college and taken home for purpose of dissection and anatomical study. They had been laid bare, and dissected from the top of the finger tips in a thoroughly professional manner and preserved in some kind of methyllated spirit, the bones emitting a faint odour, though it was probable that the parcel had been lain when it was found for some weeks. The arteries in the arm had been found with the usual liquid, consisting of an injection of arsenic, lard and wax, the decoction had the merit of congealing, and thus showing to the student the exact position of the arteries, skull too had been used in the prosecution of a doubt. The bones had been used in the prosecution of some budding surgeon, whose indiscretion in disposing of them has led to such needless investigation. The inquiries of the police confirmed this surgeon as a medical student living in Halliwell having conveyed to them that the remains were obtained from a Lancashire College, and been used for purpose of dissection.

FIFTEEN

THE BOLTON MURDER, 1901

(FROM THE *BOLTON CHRONICLE*, SATURDAY 7 DECEMBER 1901)

EXECUTION OF MCKENNA

At eight o'clock on Tuesday morning, Patrick McKenna was executed at Strangeways Gaol, Manchester, for the murder of his wife Ann McKenna, in Kestor Street, Bolton, on the 30th September. Only the gaol officials were present at the final scene.

Grim and forbidding are the surroundings of His Majesty's prison at Strangeways, and on Tuesday the great walls which form the barriers between the outside world of freedom and the captives whom a stern but righteous law has immured within them seemed to wear an added grimness from the scene that a tragedy was to be enacted in the interior. For a December day the morning broke bright and fine, although there was a Wintry shrewdness about the atmosphere which, whilst it was exhilarating to the pedestrian who moved along with rapid pace, was rather searching for those whom duty or morbid curiosity compelled to stand within the shadow of the gaol. It certainly could be described as a morning in harmony with the event, for the light shone bright upon the gruesome preparations which was being carried out within the walled enclosure, and subsequently the sun burst forth with the geniality of spring. To the residents of Strangeways – a neighbourhood which is largely a Jewish colony – an executions not uncommon occurrence, but as half-past seven approached knots of spectators, mostly of the labouring class, began to gather in the thoroughfare which commands a view of the flagstaff, and at a few minutes to eight the number had swelled to about one hundred. They were quiet and orderly, and their gaze was directed to the aperture in the roof through which the death signal was momentarily expected to rise. Up to this point the only outside indications of the impending execution were a few ominous arrivals in cabs at the gaol, these including the Under Sheriff, the prison doctor, and other officials, whose faces were the solemn gravity of men called upon to attend a dread office. A few minutes to eight a bell was heard to toll, and it was interpreted as the knell of the dying man. It strokes were mournful and few, and whilst the crowd were imagining the process of events which was transpiring unseen just beneath the flagstaff there was just perceptible movement of the cord which had hung taut and rigid from the staff, and then before one could draw breath a square of black canvas with a small coat of arms of the same sombre line in its centre, rose slowly through the aperture in the slates, then swiftly glided to the apex of the staff and calmly waved its message to the world around that the outraged law had been vindicated by the passing hence of a human soul. The crowd lingered watching the black ensign in silence, and then – as suddenly in fickle human nature moved from the sombre to the lightsome, – a little impromptu comedy enacted in the street diverted the current of their thoughts in another direction. A milk shandry had arrived at the gaol entrance, and in his hurry to deliver his supply the youth in charge fell headlong on the pavement with his overturned cans pouring their creamy contents on the pavement. The crowd of loiterers laughed, and again recollecting themselves looked once more at the flag, and then singly or in small groups moved from the scene and before long the street resumed its quiet aspect, with the policemen quietly patrolling to and fro at their measured pace as if the bright sun had witnessed no untoward event on his rising on the morning of the 3rd December.

THE SCENE WITHIN THE GAOL

As already stated the execution was a strictly private one, and the only information forthcoming respecting the final scene was that which the Governor (Major Cruikshank) furnished to the small group of reporters who waited upon him

James Billington, executioner.

after the execution had taken place. He stated that the prisoner rose early, and his last spiritual needs were attended to by the Catholic Chaplain (Father Corbistley) who celebrated High Mass from seven o'clock to 7.50, the prisoner receiving the ministrations with great devoutness. At the time stated Billington and his son commenced their dread office, McKenna submitted himself quietly to the pinioning process, and then a movement was made to the place of execution, whither McKenna was accompanied by the chaplain still administrating his consolations. The officials present also included in addition to the executor and his son, the Under Sheriff (Mr. Wright), the Governor and the prison doctor. The doomed man was taken to his position on the scaffold and the executor appears to have done his fatal duty with merciful swiftness. He drew the lever and his prisoner was immediately launched into eternity. In the words of the Governor it was done expeditiously, and the death was instantaneous. It may be added that Billington arrived on Monday afternoon at the gaol in order to carry out the preliminary arrangements, such as the erection of the scaffold. This is the first occasion on which he has executed a Bolton man, and is said to have been personally known to McKenna.

DECLARATION OF SHERIFF AND OTHERS.
SURGEON'S CERTIFICATE

Billington, who was not required at the inquest, left the prison soon after the execution was over, and proceeded to Bolton. He was questioned as to the execution, but refused to make his statement. The black flag, after hanging for about an hour, was taken down. Small knots of people for several hours assembled at the prison gates and scanned the following notices which had been placed up – I Jno. Edwards, the surgeon of His Majesty's Prison of Manchester, hereby certify that I this day examined the body of Patrick McKenna, on whom judgement of death was this day executed in the said prison, on that, and on that examination I find that the said Patrick McKenna was dead. Dated 3rd day of December, – Signed, JNO. EDWARDS.

We the undersigned hereby declare that judgement of death was this day executed on Patrick McKenna in His Majesty's Prison at Manchester, in our presence. Dated 3rd day of December, 1901 – Signed, Henry L. Wright, Under Sheriff of Lancashire, R. W. Cruickshank, Governor of the said prison, R. Corbistley, prison minister of the said prison.

THE INQUEST

At 10.30, Mr. J.F. Price (County Coroner) held an inquest on the body of the deceased in the Board Room of the Strangeways Prison. The jury having viewed the body, the evidence presented was as follows:-

R. W. Cruikshank, governor, was the first witness. He stated that the deceased man's name was Patrick McKenna, who was first received into prison on the 2nd October, on a warrant from the Justice of Bolton, to take his trial at the Assizes for the wilful murder of Ann McKenna, his wife. He was tried at the Assizes on the 13th day of November, and was sentenced to death. The sentence was that he be 'hanged by the neck until he was dead and his body buried in the precinct of the prison'. Witness was present this morning at eight o'clock when the sentence of death was duly carried out within the walls of the prison by the executioner appointed by the Sheriff, and the body viewed by the jury was the identical body of McKenna. The inquest was held within 24 hours of the execution. There was no deviation from the ordinary method of execution. Death was apparently

Churchgate, decorated for Queen Victoria's Golden Jubilee in 1887. (Image courtesy of Chris Driver)

instantaneous, and the deceased never moved. There was no unnatural circumstances. The deceased was 53, and a joiner by trade. Dr. Edwards, Medical Officer of the Prison, stated that he was present at the execution. He descended to the pit immediately afterwards, and examined the body. McKenna was then quite dead. He again examined the body in the mortuary at 10 o'clock. He formed the opinion that death was the result of strangulation and produced dislocation of the cerebral vertebrae. Death was instantaneous, and there was no movement after the body fell. The length of the drop was 6 feet and five inches. This was the whole of the evidence – The Governor asked the jury if they were satisfied that the body they viewed was that of McKenna, who was sentenced to death at the recent Assizes; that the sentence was carried out whilst in the prison in which he was confined; that an inquest had been held within 24 hours, and that the execution had been carried out in due accordance with the law? – All the jurymen assented, and a verdict in accordance with the medical testimony was returned.

THE IRONY OF COINCIDENCE

It is very curious that the two principles in the tragedy enacted at Strangeways on Tuesday should have been personally acquainted with each other. Billington and McKenna at one time, it is stated, resided in the same street at Mill Hill, and since the former assumed the responsibilities of a beerseller in Churchgate McKenna had been one of his customers. It is surely an irony of coincidence that the men should finally end their acquaintance at the scaffold, the one as the executioner of the other.

THE CRIME

It was after a long intervening absence of serious crime that on the evening of September 30th Bolton was startled by the report that a terrible murder had been committed in the Mill Hill district. The first verbal account soon unfortunately had its verification in the detailed reports published in the newspapers, and which disclosed a tragedy which, if lacking some of the elements of brutality commonly associated with some of this class, was nevertheless of a ghastly and revolting character, made up of that final combination of elements jealous, drink, and passion, which culminated in a terrible blow bringing swift death to the woman who was its victim. Within the compass was the crime which Patrick McKenna expiated with his life on Tuesday. So recent is it that a brief review rather than a recital of its details is all that is necessary by way of an epilogue to this dark domestic tragedy. The parties, McKenna and Ann McKenna, resided together in Kestor Street, and appear to have latterly led an unhappy life, part of the trouble being due to the former's addiction to drink. He was a joiner by trade, but for some time had followed the less remunerative occupation of a labourer, a fact which is said to have preyed upon his mind. He was working on the Saturday previous to this Monday night upon which the tragedy occurred, but at noon on the first mentioned day he appears to have gone on the 'spree' and continued so until he was suddenly brought to his normal state by the awful consciousness of the crime he had committed. On the Monday night the deceased woman pledged some articles at a pawnshop, and McKenna asked her for some money. She declined to give him any, and he thereupon suggested that she had been giving something to a lodger, and declared that he would cut her throat before night. He afterwards

Bolton Town Hall.

went out but subsequently returned thrice to the house, and it was on the third occasion, at five o'clock, that the crime was committed. His wife, who was in the first room, saw him approaching the house, and ran into the back room. McKenna saw her running, and following her laid hold of her by the shoulders and brought her back into the front room, threatening again that he would kill her. There was a knife lying upon the table, which was taken away, but unfortunately it was put back again. With the remark that he would kill her, he picked up the knife and thrust into her throat. He then left the house, and the woman struggled to a chair besides the door and bled to death. Prisoner hid himself in an adjoining house, where he was arrested under the stairs. When he was in charge of the constable he made a voluntary statement, in which he said: 'I went to the house without premeditation, without malice. It is horrible. She threw the knife on to table and said: "If you want to do it do it." It was done in a minute. She was launched into eternity unprepared. "She has gone to hell, if there is such a place." The proceeding which followed at the Town Hall were very expeditious owing to the clearness and compactness of the case. Within 48 hours of the committal of the offence he had been dealt with by the Coroner's jury, which found a verdict of murder, and by the Magistrates, who also sent him for trial, on the capital charge, and on the Wednesday following the Monday on which the crime was committed he left Bolton for ever.

THE TRIAL AT THE ASSIZES

On the 13th November McKenna had to face at Manchester Assizes the ordeal of the trial which was to determine his final fate, and which was conducted before Justice Bucknill. The leading counsel for the prosecution (Mr. Sutton) put the case before the jury with conspicuous fairness, and just sufficient evidence was called to establish with justice the grave indictment, after which the prisoner's counsel (Mr. Gibbons) made an earnest plea for a verdict which should save his client's life, urging that there was an absence of premeditation and of that revolting brutality which could justify a verdict of murder. The judge then laid judicially before the jury the distinction

The defence prepares to set out the case for the defence.

A judge converses with the prisoner.

which the law drew between murder and manslaughter, and also dispassionately reviewed the evidence. Prisoner had no witnesses, but it was pointed out on his behalf during the course of the trial that certain of his relatives (a brother and uncle) had been affected by insanity. There was, however, no suggestion that the prisoner himself was in such a mental condition as rendered him unfit to plead. The jury left the box to consider their verdict, a time of painful suspense for the wretched being in the dock. From their re-entry to the announcement by the foreman of their decision, the moments were for everyone in the court capable of emotion, a time of suppressed excitement. The verdict was one of 'Guilty of wilful murder,' and after this had been repeated to the prisoner, who had strained his ears in vain to catch the foreman's words, the Judge assumed the black cap, and in a slow measured terms pronounced his doom. There was one momentary gleam of light in this dark episode, and it came from the prisoner himself, in his voluntary vindication of his wife's character. Such a confession would not have come from a callous criminal.

THE EFFORTS FOR A REPRIEVE

Although the jury offered no recommendation to mercy and the Judge held out no hope to the condemned man, public feeling in Bolton has since been aroused to a considerable degree in the case, not from any sense that the sentence upon McKenna was an unjust one – for of that there could be no possible doubt entertained – but with a view to saving the life of the culprit on the ground that there were some extenuating circumstances which differentiated the case from many tragedies of this character. The Rector of St. Marie's (Father Fowler) exerted himself very greatly in the case, and Mr. Matthew Fielding (prisoner's solicitor) and Mr. Gibbons (his counsel) drew up a petition for a reprieve, which for its character the number of signatures (22,500), and the influential standing of its signatories (including the Mayor, the Borough Members, Magistrates, and representatives of the various, professions in the town) was probably unique in the town. In order to ensure its due delivery Father Fowler (armed with a letter from Mr. Shepherd-Cross, M.P, and accompanied by Mr. Geo. Harwood, M.P.) personally tendered it at the Home Office. With such a large and influential backing it was hoped the petition would have affect, but on Saturday the intelligence came that it was of no avail, and the law would have to take its course.

THE LAST EXECUTION OF A BOLTON PRISONER

Although there have been seven or eight tragedies in the town and district since, the last occasion on which a Bolton man suffered capital punishment was on December 30th 1890. The execution in that case was carried out at Kirkdale gaol.

PRISONER'S FAREWELL TO HIS RELATIVES

His crime had involved McKenna in a series of painful ordeals, one of which occurred on Saturday afternoon, when he took a last farewell of his relatives. The latter had been allowed by the gaol authorities all reasonable opportunities of visiting and corresponding with the prisoner. The scene that afternoon was exceedingly sad. Five members of the family, including prisoner's son John, his two daughters, and his brother attended at the gaol, and through the bars of the condemned cell were allowed to converse with, and finally shake hands with the prisoner in the presence of the Governor and one of the wardens.

The Governor told them that the culprit have behaved very well during his detention in gaol, and advised them not to say anything to him which would disturb him too much. He still maintained that he had no intention to kill his wife, and towards the close of the interview his feelings overcame him, and he burst into tears. His son (John), who was also crying said, 'It is hard times, dad' and he replied, 'It is,' moaning that they were never to see each other again. He seemed to have become resigned to his fate. The time allowed for the interview was only a quarter of an hour, and it was occupied chiefly by family members. They were all greatly affected when the parting came.

An assailant lunges forward, brandishing a knife...

REPORT BY A RELATIVE

One of the relatives present at the interview writes as follows:- During the interview on Saturday McKenna stated that he had no intention of doing what had occurred. He simply went to the house in search of his wife, and what followed was all done in a passion. It was a great pity the knife was on the table. He wept very bitterly, and it was indeed a sad interview. It was, I can assume you, hard times to lose mother, but it is worse to lose both. We all did our best, and now hope for the best.

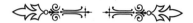

APPENDIX

WHICH COURT? CRIMINAL SOURCES

The best place to start, it you do not know which court a case appeared at, is the Criminal Registers for England and Wales 1805-1892, held at the National Archives (HO 27). The registers will tell you whether the case you are researching was held at the Assizes or Quarter Sessions. However, they do not include Magistrates Courts and the Petty Sessions. Another option is to try the digital archive of the *Manchester Guardian* to see whether the case was reported.

THE ASSIZE COURT

The most serious criminal offences were dealt with by assize courts. In Lancashire the Palatinate of Lancaster had its own jurisdiction until 1876, when it was replaced by the Northern Circuit of the assizes. Assize Court records are held at the National Archives.

Greater Manchester Police Museum holds the Calendars of Prisoners for the Assize Court of Manchester 1882-1964 (with gaps). Their address is:

Greater Manchester Police Museum, Newton Street, Manchester. M1 1ES. (Telephone: 0161 856 3287. Email: policemuseum@gmp.police.uk. Their website can be found http://www.gmp.police.uk/mainsite/pages/history.htm)

QUARTER SESSIONS COURTS

The Quarter Session Court dealt with less serious crimes than Assize Courts. It usually met four times a year. The Borough of Manchester was granted its own Court and Quarter Sessions on 1 April 1839. The Manchester Quarter Sessions' area of jurisdiction was the Borough/City of Manchester.

Before 1839 Manchester cases were tried at the Lancashire Quarter Sessions (Hundred of Salford). The Quarter Session records for Lancashire are held at the Lancashire Record Office, which hold microfilm copies of the order books in the Microfilm Unit 1626-1888 (ref: MF211-2770. Also held are some Calendars of Prisoners tried at the Quarter Sessions of the County of Lancashire (Hundred of Salford), 1821-1840 (ref: L27). Records are held of the Borough / City of Manchester Quarter Sessions (ref: M116). The Quarter Sessions files 1839-1954 (ref: M116/2/4/1-662) consist of mainly indictments, but also include some minutes, calendars of prisoners, previous convictions, costs, legal aid certificates, jury lists, coroner's lists and expenses and orders relating roads. The names of prisoners in these files for 1839 March 1911 have been indexed. This index is available in the archives catalogue (put ref: M116/2/4 in the Re No field and the surname you are researching in the 'Any Text' field). Printed calendars of prisoners 1851 - 1852, 1882-1884 and 1903-1956 (ref: M116/2/3/1-30) are also held.

The following boroughs in the Manchester region also had their own Courts of Quarter Sessions:

> Borough / City of Salford (granted 1890). Records 1890-1971 (incomplete) are held by Greater Manchester County Record Office. Borough of Bolton (granted 1838). Records are held by Bolton Archives. Borough of Wigan (granted 1866). Records are held by Wigan Archives. Borough of Oldham records 1939-1972 are held by the Greater Manchester County Record Office.

Those areas of Greater Manchester which were traditionally part of Lancashire and did not have their own Quarter Sessions would have been under the jurisdiction of the Lancashire Quarter Sessions (Salford Hundred). Those areas of Greater Manchester which were traditionally part of Cheshire would have been under the jurisdiction of the Chester Quarter Sessions. The records of this court are held by Cheshire Record Office.

MANCHESTER COURT LEET

The Court Leet of the Manor of Manchester was the ancient Court for the Manor of Manchester. It was abolished in 1846. The Court Leet Records of the Manor Manchester 1552-1846 have been published and copies are available in Manchester Archives and Local Studies (352.042 M4).

CROWN COURT OF MANCHESTER

In 1956 the City of Manchester Quarter Sessions and Assize Court were replaced by the Crown Court. This court holds calendars of prisoners for the Crown Court of Manchester in two volumes, 1956-1960 (ref: M545).

CITY OF MANCHESTER PETTY SESSIONS (MAGISTRATES COURT / POLICE COURT)

Petty Sessions Courts met daily and dealt with minor crimes, licensing, juvenile offenders and civil matters such as bastardy, child maintenance and adoption. Records are held for the City of Manchester Petty Sessions Court, 1839-1970 (ref: M117). The Manchester Petty Sessions area of jurisdiction was the Borough / City of Manchester. Petty Sessions were also responsible for victuallers' licenses and licensing records for the Borough / City of Manchester from 1869-1960s. Please note these records only cover the area of the Borough / City of Manchester (as it was at the time).

MANCHESTER COUNTY PETTY SESSIONAL DIVISION (MAGISTRATE COURT)

A growth in population of Manchester and Salford led to the formation of the Manchester County Petty Sessions Division in 1868. It met at the newly built Strangeways Court. Lancaster Record Office holds records for this division (ref: PSMA). The Greater Manchester County Record Office also holds some records for this court (ref: A/TRAFF).

Botany Bay, 1825. Many convicts were transported to Australia where life was harsh and unforgiving.

SALFORD AND MANCHESTER COURT OF RECORD

Salford Hundred Court was originally the ancient Court for Salford Wapentake or Hundred, covering one of the six administrative areas of the county. It continued to be held until the nineteenth century with the Molyneuxs, the Earls of Sefton, as hereditary stewards. By then, however, its only residual jurisdiction outside the borough of Salford was where townships had no Court Leets of their own; it elected constables and dealt with minor nuisances. Its principal business in Salford after the establishment of the Police Commissioners had dwindled to the appointment of the Borough reeve and other officials. Concurrently however, a sitting of the court for the trial of civil actions for debt or damage under 40s was held every three weeks. In 1846, this Court was constituted a Court of Record and its jurisdiction extended to £50.

In 1868, the Court was amalgamated with the Manchester Court of Record which had its origins in Manchester's Charter of Incorporation, 1838. At first, the jurisdiction of the latter court had been limited to £20, but in 1845, it was increased to £50. The new Court had jurisdiction in personal actions only and by 1911 its area became limited to the area of the Manchester and Salford County Courts. The Court was abolished on the 31st December 1971.

Manchester Archives holds the following records of the above court (ref: M123): Acts of Parliament and rules of Manchester Borough Court of Record and Salford Hundred Court of Record 1845-1971; Other Acts of Parliament and Rules 1869-1920; Manchester City Council 1935-1936; Government Inquiries 1911-1969; Administrative Papers 1852-1956; Papers concerning official of the court 1858-1926; Attorneys. Detailing the names of those serving the court [1838?]-1964; Business of the Court 1916-1971 including the names of those appearing before the court; Precedents and miscellaneous documents 1862-1971. Many of its earlier records were destroyed by enemy action during World War II.

MANCHESTER COUNTY COURT

County Courts were formed in 1846 to deal with small debts and other civil claims. No records appear to have survived of Manchester County Court.

MANCHESTER CORONERS COURT

Unfortunately, coroner's records frequently have been destroyed. This is certainly the case with the records of the coroner for the city of Manchester, where the only nineteenth century records to survive are witnesses depositions for the dates 22nd August 185-24th December 1852, (ref M381/1/1/1-2). Greater Manchester County Record Office holds twentieth century coroner's records, namely indexes 1918-1998 and inquests 1959-1998. Coroner's records are closed for 75 years, and permission to see records less than 75 years old would have to be obtained from the Manchester Coroner, and is only given in exceptional circumstances. In the absence of coroner's records, a report of any inquest conducted by the coroner for the city of Manchester might be found in local newspapers. A scrapbook of newspaper cuttings for the period 1900-1938 (ref M381/2), mostly concerned with coroner's cases may be seen. It is not clear how complete the scrapbook is and, in the absence of an index, the court concerned will not search for items on your behalf.

STRANGEWAYS GAOL

Strangeways Prison in Southall Street, Manchester was built to replace New Bailey Prison in Salford which closed in June 1868. It acted as the County Gaol for the Hundred of Salford (south-east Lancashire). It was renamed Her Majesty's Prison, Manchester in the 1990s. Manchester Archives holds the following records for this prison:

Female Registers, 1868-1875; Female Description Books, 1867-1879; Males Registers, 1869-1879 (with gaps); Male and Female Register (Small Debts), Dec 1879-Dec 1881. Felony Register – Bolton and Salford Sessions and Manchester Assizes (Male) Jan 1853-Dec 1872 (ref: M600/4/1). This is probably for New Bailey Prison and Strangeways Prison.

If you find an ancestor in Strangeways do not automatically assume they would have been tried at the Manchester Quarter Sessions. The Manchester Quarter Sessions only covered the City of Manchester and Strangeways Prison took prisoners from all over south-east Lancashire. It is more likely that they would have been tried at the Assize Court – or ,if it was a short custodial sentence, at their local magistrates or Quarter Session Court.

PRISON RECORDS

As the borough of Manchester had no gaol in 1839, agreement was made with the county magistrates of Lancashire that persons sentenced for up to six months should be housed at the New Bailey Prison, Salford, while longer term prisoners went to the County Gaol at Lancashire. Manchester Archives holds the following records for New Bailey Prison.

General Registers (Male), 1859-1869; Nominal Register (Small Debts – Male and Female), Sept 1863-19 Nov 1864, 28 Aug-29 Oct 1868; Female and Male Register, 1847-1872; Female Register, Aug 1862-July 1867; Female Description Books, 1859-1867. The records of Lancashire Prison are held by the National Archives, but Lancashire Record Office hold microfilm copies of these.

BELLE VUE PRISON (OR MANCHESTER BOROUGH GAOL / MANCHESTER CITY GAOL)

Hyde Road, West Gorton was opened in 1849 by the Borough of Manchester. It was a short-term jail, but it proved inadequate and some prisoners were still sent to the New Bailey. It was demolished in 1892. The majority of prisoners were tried at the Manchester Magistrates Court or the Manchester Quarter Sessions. Manchester Archives holds the following records for this prison: General Registers (Male and Female), 1850-1880 (some gaps).

USEFUL WEBSITES FOR TRACING PRISONERS AND CRIMINALS

Newspapers are a good way to trace details of a trial. The *Manchester Guardian* can now be searched online at http://www.guardian.co.uk/archive. Most newspapers are held but only the *Manchester Guardian* is indexed.

The British convict transportation registers 1787-1867 database at http://www.slq.qld.gov.au/into/fh/convicts has been compiled from the British Home Office (HO) records. You can find details for over 123,000 of the estimated 160,000 convicts transported to Australia in the eighteenth and nineteenth centuries – names, term of years, transport ships and more.

The proceedings of the Old Bailey 1674-1913 are available on-line at http://www.oldbaileyonline.org The Old Bailey is England's most important crown court. This court can try crimes from any part of the country.

Manchester Family History Research contains a lot of good information about prison records, court records, the Manchester Martyrs and also includes a list of Manchester and Lancashire strays in Millbank Prison, London. http://www.manchester-family-history-research.co.uk.

A prisoner is secured following his arrest.

Other titles published by The History Press

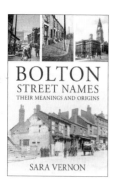

Bolton Street Names: Their Meanings and Origins
SARA VERNON

Take a fascinating trip around Bolton with this comprehensive etymological guide to its highways and byways.

Discover the origins of the peculiarly named 'Bowkers Row' and 'Thweat Street', delve into the lives of some of Bolton's famous residents commemorated in the road names of their town, and find out about the numerous buildings and industries that also left their mark on Bolton's streets.

978 0 7524 4652 3

Hanged at Manchester
STEVE FIELDING

For decades the high walls of Manchester's Strangeways Prison have contained some of England's most infamous criminals. Until hanging was abolished in the 1960s it was also the main centre of execution for convicted murderers from all parts of the north west.

Fully illustrated with rare photographs, documents and news-cuttings, *Hanged at Manchester* is bound to appeal to anyone interested in the darker side of this area's history

978 0 7509 5052 7

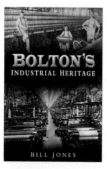

Bolton's Industrial Heritage
BILL JONES

Bolton was built on the cotton industry with, at its peak, over 200 mills in the town: the last closed in 2002 after a gradual decline throughout the twentieth century. This illustrated book includes information about the transport infrastructure that made all this industrial activity practicable, as well as essential public utilities.

978 0 7509 4442 7

Greater Manchester Murders
ALAN HAYHURST

Contained within the pages of this book are the stories behind some of the most notorious murders in the history of Greater Manchester. They include the case of notorious cat burglar, Charlie Peace, who killed twenty-year-old PC Nicholas Cook in Seymour Grove, and only confessed when he had already been sentenced to death for another murder; Kay Howarth, who faked a suicide note by his victim; and Harry Hammond Swindells, a convicted murderer who escaped from prison only to be recaptured and hanged.

978 0 7509 5091 6

Visit our website and discover thousands of other History Press books.
www.thehistorypress.co.uk

The History Press